Nathaniel William Wraxall

Memoirs of the Kings of France, of the Race of Valois

Vol. I

Nathaniel William Wraxall

Memoirs of the Kings of France, of the Race of Valois
Vol. I

ISBN/EAN: 9783743401747

Manufactured in Europe, USA, Canada, Australia, Japa

Cover: Foto ©ninafisch / pixelio.de

Manufactured and distributed by brebook publishing software (www.brebook.com)

Nathaniel William Wraxall

Memoirs of the Kings of France, of the Race of Valois

MEMOIRS

OF THE

KINGS OF FRANCE,

OF THE

RACE OF VALOIS.

INTERSPERSED WITH INTERESTING ANECDOTES.

TO WHICH IS ADDED,

A TOUR

THROUGH THE WESTERN, SOUTHERN, AND INTERIOR PROVINCES OF FRANCE,

IN A SERIES OF LETTERS.

By NATH^l. WRAXALL, Junr. Efq;

IN TWO VOLUMES.

VOL. I.

LONDON:
PRINTED FOR EDWARD AND CHARLES DILLY.
M.DCC.LXXVII,

TO THE
EARL OF HILLSBOROUGH.

MY LORD,

IF the memoirs and anecdotes of illustrious men have, in all ages, been interesting to mankind in general, how much more so must they be to those who move in the same sphere, and seem to be in a manner connected with them by rank, occupation, and character?

It was the sense of this peculiar propriety, which first made me desirous of addressing the following sheets to your Lordship.

What

What other motives concurred in fuggefting the wifh, I am withheld from expreffing, by the apprehenfion of offending that delicacy which never fails to characterife great minds, and which leaves me only the liberty of declaring in general terms, the fincere refpect and admiration, with which I have the honour to be,

 My Lord,

  Your Lordfhip's

   moft obedient,

    humble fervant,

London, New Bond-ftreet,
November 22, 1776.

N. WRAXALL, Junr.

CONTENTS

OF THE

FIRST VOLUME.

CHAPTER THE FIRST.

Introduction, on the different genius of English and French history.—Situation of France at the death of John, and accession of Charles the fifth.—Character of Charles the Bad king of Navarre.—Declension of the English affairs.—Death of Charles the fifth. Character.—Charles the sixth succeeds.— Disorders under the regency of the duke of Anjou.—The king becomes of age.—Appearance of the spectre in the wood of Mans.— Charles's madness.—Characters of the Queen, and duke of Orleans.—King's relapse at a masquerade.—Disorders in the State.— Assassination of the duke of Orleans.—Long anarchy which succeeds.—Henry the fifth lays claim to the crown.—Louis the dauphin dies.—John, second dauphin dies.—

The Queen's intrigues with the duke of Burgundy.—His affaffination.—Rapid fucceffes of Henry the fifth.—Marriage.—Death.—Charles the fixth expires.—Reflections. ——— ——— Page 1

CHAPTER THE SECOND.

Political condition of France.—Character of John duke of Bedford.—Acceffion and diftreffes of Charles the feventh.—Appearance of the Maid of Orleans.—Character of Agnes Soreille.—Deaths of the Queen dowager, and duke of Bedford.—Louis the Dauphin's treafonable practices, and flight.—Death of Agnes Soreille.—Circumftances of it.—Englifh ultimately driven out of France.—Dauphin's difobedience,—Oppreffions, and retreat into Burgundy.—Charles's fruitlefs attempts to gain poffeffion of his perfon.—The king's illnefs. —Death.—Character. ——— Page 51

CHAPTER THE THIRD.

Louis the eleventh's character, and commencement of his reign.—Interview with Henry king of Caftile.—Louis's violence and oppreffions.—League of the public good.—Acceffion and character of Charles laft duke of Burgundy.—Interview of Peronne.—

CONTENTS.

Peronne.—King's imprisonment and terrors.—Death of Charles duke of Berri.— Interview with Edward the fourth at Pecquigni.—Louis's insidious policy.—The duke of Burgundy's attempts on Switzerland, Battle of Nancy, and death.— Burgundy re-united to France.—Conclusion of Louis's reign.—Cruelties.—First stroke of an apoplexy.—His pilgrimage.— His encreasing severity.—Minute circumstances of his illness.—Death.—Character. —Mistresses. ——— Page 76

CHAPTER THE FOURTH.

Accession of Charles the eighth.—Character of the regent, Anne Lady of Beaujeu.— Her administration.— Attempts on the duchy of Bretagne.—The duke of Orleans's intrigues and flight.—His imprisonment. —Marriage of Anne of Bretagne to the king.—The duchy united to the crown.— Termination of the regency.—Charles's opening character.—He is inflamed with schemes of conquest.— Attack on the kingdom of Naples.—Romantic expedition. —His march— Uninterrupted train of victory—Coronation—Return.—Battle of Fornoua.—Charles abandons himself to pleasures.—Naples lost.—New plans of invasion.—Renounced.—The king's change and sudden death.—Circumstances of it.— Character. ——— Page 116

CHAPTER THE FIFTH.

Louis the twelfth's accession and character.— His divorce, and marriage with Anne of Bretagne.—Conquest of Milan, and imprisonment of Ludovico Sforza.—Recovery of Naples, and division of it with Ferdinand of Arragon—Perfidy of that prince. — Gonsalvo de Cordova drives out the French.—Magnanimity of Louis.—His dangerous illness.—Death of Isabella of Castile.—Julius the second's accession to the papacy.—Character.—League of Cambray.—Death of the Cardinal of Amboise. —Julius's ambition and successes.—Gaston de Foix appears.—His victories.—Battle of Ravenna.—Death—Circumstances.— French driven out of Italy.—Julius dies. —Leo the tenth accedes to the pontificate. —Illness and death of Anne of Bretagne.—Her character.—The king's grief. Marriage of Francis Count d'Angoulesme to the princess Claude.—State of the court.— Louis's marriage.—Illness. — Death.— Character. ——— Page 145

CHAPTER THE SIXTH.

Accession and Character of Francis the first. —Character of Louisa Countess d'Angoulesme.—

lefme.—Battle of Marignano.—Death of Ferdinand of Arragon and the Emperor Maximilian.—Interview of Francis and Henry the eighth.—Commencement of the wars between the King and Emperor.—Character of Charles of Bourbon.—Of Bonnivet.—Death of Leo the tenth.—Milan lost.—Execution of Semblençai.—Conspiracy of the Constable of Bourbon.—Minute circumstances of his treason and flight.—Death of the Queen.—The Admiral Bonnivet enters Italy.—Bourbon lays siege to Marseilles.—Francis pursues him over the Alps.—Battle of Pavia. Minute enumeration of the circumstances of the King's imprisonment.—Death of Bonnivet.—Francis's confinement, and removal to Madrid.—Measures of the regent.—The King's rigorous captivity.—Illness.—Visit of the Duchess of Alençon, his sister.—Release.—Entry into his dominions.—Commencement of the Duchess of Estampes' favour, ——   Page 183

CHAPTER THE SEVENTH.

Treaty of Madrid violated.—War renewed between Francis and the Emperor.—Unsuccessful attack of Naples.—Death of Lautrec.—Peace of Cambray.—Marriage of Francis to Eleanor of Portugal.—Magnificence

CONTENTS.

ficence of the King—Death of his mother Louisa.—Interview of Marseilles.—Marriage of the Duke of Orleans to Catherine of Medicis.—War renewed.—The Emperor enters Provence.—Death of Francis the Dauphin.—Circumstances of it.—His character.—Reflections.—The Emperor retreats into Italy.—Marriage of James the fifth to the Princess Magdalen.—Character of Anne de Montmorenci.—Interviews of Nice and Aigues-Mortes.— Story of the cave in Dauphiné.—Francis's amours.—Indisposition, and consequent change.—Visit of the Emperor.—Alteration of the ministers.—Third war.—Description of the court.—Battle of Cerizoles.—The Emperor enters Picardy.—Intrigues of the Duchess of Estampes.—Peace concluded.—Death of the Duke of Orleans.—Circumstances.—Character.—Death of the Count d'Enguien.—Parties formed in the court.—Francis's illness.—Circumstances—Dying admonitions to the Dauphin.—Death.—Character. —— Page 235

CHAPTER THE EIGHTH.

Character of Henry the second.—Changes in the state.—Diana de Poitiers.—Her character.—Romantic attachment of the King.--Disgrace of the Duchess of Estampes.—Duel

CONTENTS.

—*Duel of Jarnac and La Chataigneraie.*—*Insurrections in Guyenne.*—*Persecution of the Protestants.*—*Death of Margaret of Valois Queen of Navarre.*—*Character.*—*War renewed between Henry and the Emperor.*—*Catherine of Medicis left regent.*—*Siege of Metz.*—*War continued.*—*The Emperor abdicates.*—*Power of Diana Duchess of Valentinois.*—*The Duke of Guise sent against Naples.*—*Battle of St. Quentin.*—*Capture of Calais.*—*Marriage of Francis the Dauphin, to Mary of Scotland.*—*Circumstances.*—*Peace concluded.*—*Carousals of the court.*—*The King's unexpected death.*—*Enumeration of the circumstances which attended it.*—*Character of Henry the second.*—*Mistresses.*—*Reflections.* — Page 296

CHAPTER THE NINTH.

State of the kingdom at the death of Henry the second.—*Character of the Duke of Guise*—*of the Cardinal of Lorrain*—*of the King of Navarre*—*of the Prince of Condé.*—*Catherine of Medicis.*—*Her character*—*person*—*political conduct.*—*Disgrace of the Duchess of Valentinois.*—*Accession of Francis the second.*—*Power of the Guises.*—*The King's feeble health.*—*Assassination of Minard.*—*Conspiracy of Amboise.*—

CONTENTS.

Amboife.—Defeated.—Horrible executions.—The Prince of Condé fufpected.—Convocation of Fontainbleau.—The King of Navarre and Prince of Condé arrive at court.—They are arrefted.—Trial of the latter.—Francis's illnefs.—Condé condemned.—Intrigues and cabals of Catherine of Medicis.—Death of Francis the fecond.—Circumftances.—Character.—Funerals.—Arrival of Montmorenci.—Releafe of Condé. ——— Page 352

MEMOIRS

MEMOIRS

OF THE

KINGS OF FRANCE, &c.

CHAPTER THE FIRST.

Introduction, on the different genius of English and French history.—Situation of France at the death of John, and accession of Charles the fifth.—Character of Charles the Bad, king of Navarre.—Declension of the English affairs.—Death of Charles the fifth—Character.—Charles the sixth succeeds.—Disorders under the regency of the duke of Anjou.—The king becomes of age.—Story of the spectre in the wood of Mans.—Charles's madness.—Characters of the queen, and duke of Orleans.—King's relapse at a masquerade.--Disorders in the State.--Assassination of the duke of Orleans.—Long anarchy which succeeds.—Henry the fifth lays claim to the crown.—Louis, the dauphin, dies.—John, second dauphin, dies.—The queen's intrigues with the duke of Burgundy—His assassination.—Rapid successes of Henry the fifth—Marriage—Death.—Charles the sixth expires.—Reflections.

THE history of France may be considered as abounding more in those interesting scenes which touch the heart, than any other.

The annals of England are bolder, and marked with stronger colours; but, like the genius of the nation, they are austere and gloomy. Few of those pleasing and elegant anecdotes occur, which soften the horror of battles, and open the gentler sources of entertainment. The long wars and alternate massacres of the two houses of York and Lancaster, were followed by the capricious tyranny of the family of Tudor. Even

KINGS OF FRANCE, &c. 3

Even Elizabeth's reign, juftly renowned for policy and wifdom, is not comparable, for refinement and cultivation of manners, to the court of Catharine of Medicis. The efforts of a paffion for liberty, however noble and juftifiable in themfelves, mingled with the frenzy of fanaticifm, impeded the entrance of thofe humanizing arts which polifh fociety, during the greater part of the feventeenth century; and Charles the fecond, educated in foreign countries, and habituated to more courtly climes, firft introduced that fpirit of gallantry, which was unknown before to the nation, or at leaft but faintly characterifed it.

The French hiftory, on the contrary, is exuberant in thofe ftrokes and characters which bring the fovereign immediately to our view, and even diveft him of all that fplendor or dignity, which ufually veils him from obfervation. The little weakneffes of the heart, the trefpaffes of paffion, how infinitely do they engage! We contemplate ourfelves, we pity, and we
B 2   forgive.

forgive.—Why are Francis the firſt, and Henry the fourth, ſo peculiarly objects of the attachment of every feeling reader? Becauſe they were diſtinguiſhed by thoſe amiable and engaging foibles which ſerve to contraſt the virtues of the warrior and the king, which nature has almoſt conſtantly and inſeparably interwoven in animated and exalted boſoms. We like to quit the council-board, or the plain of carnage and deſolation, to follow the man, and behold him in the retirements of private life.

From this principle it is, that Memoirs, though leſs noble and auguſt than Hiſtory, are yet generally more juſt to nature, and intereſt us in a livelier degree. Confined to a narrower ſphere, but diffuſe and minute, they ſatisfy the reſtleſs curioſity of the mind, to know thoſe trivial and unimportant tranſactions of the individual, which Hiſtory diſdains to enumerate, and paſſes over in ſilence.

In theſe ſources of information, the French are as profuſe, as we ſeem to have been

been barren and unproductive: nor are the amours and intrigues of the court of James the first better known than those of Francis the first, though posterior by near a century.

There is, however, a point, beyond which a liberal but corrected curiosity carries not its researches. The events of the eleventh, twelfth, and thirteenth centuries are wrapped in too grofs a barbarism, and obscured by too profound an ignorance, to merit the pains or repay the trouble of an elaborate search. Scarce any materials are procurable; scarce any of the great actuating motives which then influenced the princes or people exist in any shape at present; scarce any deductions are applicable to these times, from the conduct or policy of those. As knowledge and letters broke in upon this darkness, every thing rises in its effect upon the mind, and becomes of importance. The objects swell to the view, and are more intimately discernable.—There is, perhaps, no exact and precise æra at which to date this alteration. I cannot extend it higher than the acceſſion of Philip de Valois; to bring it down to that of Charles the ſeventh may be too ſevere.—Let us begin with the reign of Charles the fifth.

I pretend not to give any accurate picture of kings or governments: I boaſt not to throw many new lights on hiſtory; I mean not to enter into a chronological narration of facts.—My wiſh is to place before the reader thoſe ſtriking qualities of the ſucceſſive princes, which bring them forward to the eye, and characterize the manners of the age in which they flouriſhed; to make him acquainted with the chief miniſters, or miſtreſſes, or generals, who acted the ſecond parts under them; to allow myſelf the fulleſt liberty of reflection, of cenſure, of admiration, uninfluenced by preſcription, prejudice, or country.

If we ſurvey the ſituation of France at the period with which I have choſen to begin,

begin, it prefents a fcene of defolation, and almoft of anarchy. The unjuft pretenfions of Edward the third of England to the crown, had involved the kingdom in blood and ruin. If he did not attain the complete gratification of his ambition, his glory at leaft was fatiated by the captivity of John; and the peace of Bretigny had reftored to him all thofe provinces which his anceftors had poffeffed in Guyenne and Gafcony. His fon, the Black Prince, yet dreadful from the fields of Crecy and of Poitiers, held his court in thefe dominions. He was ftill in the prime of manhood, and his character, adorned with all the fhining qualities of a warrior and a fovereign, fpread terror to the remoteft confines of the French monarchy.

Charles the Bad, king of Navarre, had already been active in all the commotions of the preceding reign; he had pretenfions to the crown in right of his mother Jane, daughter of Louis the tenth, and his turbulent and difcontented fpirit induced him to form alliances of the clofeft nature with the Englifh. Nature had endowed him with all thofe talents and qualifications, which, under the guidance of a vicious heart, are eminently pernicious. Munificent and generous, he captivated the multitude. Verfed in all the arts of addrefs, and even of eloquence to varnifh over his crimes, he had boldnefs enough to perpetrate the moft atrocious. An avowed and inveterate enemy to Charles, he had given him poifon when dauphin, and though the effects of it were retarded, they yet terminated in his death fome years afterwards. Fickle and perfidious, he violated even his interefts to gratify his paffions, and trampled on the laws of confanguinity, of patriotifm, and of honour.

Bands of defperate banditti, to whom the late wars had given birth, and whom the peace had rendered unneceffary, overran the provinces, and added to the general confufion. The lands lay defert and uncultivated; a plague had fwept away prodigious numbers of the people; and the

KINGS OF FRANCE, &c.

the taxes, which the ranfom of the late king and the diforders of the ftate had encreafed to an unprecedented degree, tended to produce a fpirit of revolt and difaffection among them.

Charles had only attained his twenty-fixth year when he afcended the throne, but he had been educated in the fchool of great princes, adverfity. Inftructed by the fatal experience of his father and grandfather, he ftudioufly avoided thofe errors into which their prefumption and rafhnefs had led them.

A train of victory and conqueft had raifed the courage of the Englifh nation, and depreffed the genius of France. Two able and powerful princes commanded them, both in the vigor of their age. Though the ftorm had fpent its force, it was not yet fubfided, nor did any apparent decline in their affairs mark the moment when they might be attacked with fuccefs. Charles knew how to adopt that wary and temporifing policy, which peculiarly diftinguifhes ftatefmen born to retrieve the affairs of

empires,

empires, and which almost always finally attains its ends. It is not fortune, but wisdom, that disposes of the events of human life.

A circumstance which at first seemed to carry the English glory to the greatest heighth, opened to Charles the occasion he so much desired, and enabled him from the recesses of the Louvre to regain without a battle what both his predecessors had lost. Pedro, surnamed the Cruel and the Wicked, reigned in Castile. He had put his queen to death by poison, though young and beautiful, and virtuous, to gratify a mistress to whom he was enslaved. He had murdered one of his brothers, and attempted the lives of the others. Henry de Trastemare, the eldest of these, weary of the tyrant's excesses, and pushed by despair, fled into France. Charles the fifth received him with open arms, lent him a general and troops, with which he returned into Spain, and by whose assistance he dispossessed his rival.

Pedro, detested and odious even to foreigners,

reigners, endeavoured in vain to find an asylum in Portugal; and after wandering some time in Galicia, he embarked for Bourdeaux, to implore the protection and assistance of the prince of Wales. Fond of military fame, and flattered by the title of restorer or dethroner of kings, in an evil hour the prince consented. He marched across the Pyrenees, and met his antagonist in the plains of Navarette. Victory, which still waited on him, declared in his favour. He replaced Pedro on the throne, and was repaid with that ingratitude which he ought to have expected. Scarce could he carry back to France the half of his troops, thinned by distempers, unrecompensed, and discontented. He himself could not escape the attacks of a disease, which, though not immediately mortal, incapacitated him for those feats of arms, and that exertion of personal prowess, which had rendered him so eminent and renowned.

Bertrand du Guesclin, only the second captain of his age while the Black Prince could

could bear the weight of armour; who had been twice his prifoner, and whom he had fet free from a magnanimous contempt of his capacity, now came forward. Charles put into his hand the conftable's fword, and ordered him to unfheath it againft the enemies of France. In vain did the conqueror of Poitiers attempt to fupport the great name which he had acquired in war. Vainly, with an indignant pride, did he threaten to attend his fovereign lord, who fummoned him as vaffal, with fixty thoufand men, and a helmet on his head. Debilitated, feeble, and depreffed by ficknefs, he made only fome ineffectual efforts to ftem the torrent of adverfe fortune. His death foon followed; and the minority which took place under his fon, left Charles and du Guefclin an almoft undifputed conqueft.

In a few years all the victories of Edward were rendered abortive; and of the vaft dominions which he had acquired, only Calais, Bourdeaux, and Bayonne remained to his fucceffor. France had re-acquired

KINGS OF FRANCE, &c. 13

quired her natural and ancient, afcendant; a wife and vigorous adminiftration fucceeding to the paft convulfions, produced effects the moft beneficial. Order and tranquillity began to refume their feat in the provinces from which they had fo long been banifhed, and the houfe of Valois no longer held a precarious throne; when Charles expired in the prime of his age. Hiftorians attribute it to the effects of that poifon which the king of Navarre had adminiftered to him many years before, and the confequences of which a German phyfician had protracted in fome degree, by an iffue in his arm, which he at the fame time predicted muft be followed by death whenever it clofed. Whether this ftory does not carry with it a certain air of the marvellous, or whether poifons can be thus delayed and mitigated, may perhaps appear doubtful *. Whatever was the

caufe,

* All the cotemporary writers agree in the affertion, that the king of Navarre adminiftered poifon to the dauphin; and that it was fo violent as to caufe his

hair,

cause, the effect was ruinous and destructive to the kingdom. With the king expired the guardian genius of the monarchy; and France, rescued by his wisdom, relapsed into all the miseries she had previously experienced.

It is unnecessary to draw the portrait of Charles the fifth: it is beheld in the epitome of his reign. His sagacity, his masterly and tempered policy, were superior to all the eclat of military ardor. He foresaw the evils which must inevitably

hair, nails, and the external skin to come off. The emperor Charles the fourth sent him a physician, who in some degree suspended the progress, and diminished the mortal tendency of the venom, by opening a fistula in his arm. Charles the Bad himself survived the king of France about seven years, and perished by a death equally singular and deplorable, in a very advanced age.—He was attacked with the leprosy, a disease, in that century, common through all Europe. His physicians had ordered him to be wrapped in bandages of linen previously steeped in brandy and sulphur. A spark of fire accidentally falling on him, he was so miserably burnt, before his attendants could extinguish it, that he expired at Pampelona only three days after.

from

KINGS OF FRANCE, &c. 15

enfue to the ftate from the fituation of affairs, but he forefaw without being able to redrefs them. He had intended to veft the regency in the queen, one of the moft accomplifhed and virtuous princeffes of her time; but death deprived the kingdom of this refource; and Bertrand du Guefclin, from whofe valour and conduct the ftate might have drawn infinite advantages, was now no more. Perhaps no death was ever more fatal to France, except that of Henry the fecond, which opened the wars of Calvinifm and of the League; nor can it be doubted, that if Charles had lived a few years longer, he would have obtained the moft complete fuperiority over the Englifh, whom the vices of Richard the fecond involved in all the confufion of civil difcord.

Charles the fixth, who fucceeded, was only twelve years of age; and as it was therefore neceffary to appoint a regent, the late king, confcious that his brother the duke of Anjou had the jufteft claim

to

from proximity of blood, nominated him to that charge previous to his death; and his firſt care was to aſſume the power: but as the perſon of the prince and the care of his education were conſigned to other hands, theſe divided and jarring intereſts ſoon broke out into open animoſity. The regent ſeems to be marked by no other qualities than an unbounded rapacity, and an inordinate ambition; vices too common to perſons of exalted ſtations to form any great diſcriminating character!

The duke of Berri, third ſon of John, was a prince of mean abilities, and whom the ſuperior talents of his competitors in adminiſtration ever retained in a ſort of ſubordination and inferiority.

Philip the youngeſt, duke of Burgundy, was already celebrated by his valour, and powerful from his dominions. The favourite of his father, by whoſe ſide he was taken priſoner at the battle of Poitiers, when his other ſons deſerted him; John had diſtinguiſhed his courage and attachment by a reward worthy a ſovereign, the
inveſtiture

KINGS OF FRANCE, &c.

inveftiture of Burgundy, the greateft fief dependant on the crown. In this facrifice to affection, he violated the rules of found policy, and laid the foundation of ills which his defcendants had caufe to regret. Superadded to a dukedom in poffeffion, Philip had a vaft territory in expectation by his marriage with the heirefs of the count of Flanders; and as he was eminent for intrepidity, and not defective in capacity, he formed an infuperable barrier to the power which the regent claimed, and attempted to exercife. The authority of this latter was, however, of fhort duration, and that luft of dominion which diftinguifhed him, was the immediate caufe of his ignominy and death.

The diffolute and voluptuous Joan, defcended from Charles of Anjou, brother of St. Louis, reigned in Naples. Charles de Durazzo, her relation, whom fhe had adopted as her fucceffor, and whom fhe had bound by every obligation to gratitude, by an act of the bafeft inhumanity depofed and murdered his benefactrefs: previous

vious to her death, the unfortunate queen called to her refcue the duke of Anjou, and inftituted him to the fucceffion.

Inflamed with defire to poffefs the diadem devolved to him, the regent redoubled his exactions on the people, feized on all the treafures which the late king had concealed in the walls of the caftle of Melun; and encouraged by the Antipope, from whom he received the crown at Avignon, he marched his troops into Italy, confifting of thirty thoufand cavalry—but the Neapolitan prince, too wife to hazard a battle, and fkilled in all the duplicity of Italian negotiation, deluded his rival by challenges which he never meant to fulfil, and protracted the execution of them till famine and difeafe began to wafte his forces. Surrounded, harraffed, and continually purfued by a fuperior army, the duke of Anjou was at length reduced to fuch extreme diftrefs, that of all the immenfe treafures which he had carried from France, he had only one fuit of arms made of painted ftuff, and a fingle cup of filver.

Dejected

Dejected with such a series of calamities, forgotten in France, and unassisted by his brothers, he at length sunk under the pressure, and died in Calabria in the deepest want, and almost abandoned.

If we turn our view to France, we shall find all the disorders and oppressions which usually attend on minorities.—The dukes of Berri and Burgundy, greedy of power, and using it to the injury of the state, gave rise by their exactions to sedition and tumult. The young king, whom his father had begun to train in sentiments of virtue and greatness, neglected in his education, studiously kept from an acquaintance with the affairs of his kingdom, and only taught to follow the chace, or immersed in debauchery, promised no redress to these misfortunes. His heart was generous, beneficent, and friendly; he loved his people, he wished, and even endeavoured to give them proofs of this disposition: his understanding, though much uncultivated, and left to unfold itself without any aid, yet appears to have been clear,

clear, juft, and manly. As he approached to years of maturity, the authority of his uncles diminifhed; and when he firft affumed the reins of government, he conciliated the affections of his people, by depriving the duke of Berri of the government of Languedoc, which he had greatly abufed, and by the abfolute difmiffion of the duke of Burgundy.

The kingdom began to recover from the evils of a divided legiflature, when an accident the moft extraordinary and deplorable renewed and aggravated them——I mean, the king's madnefs. The circumftances of it are very curious. We muft go back a little, to trace them to the fource.

During the extreme diftreffes to which Louis duke of Anjou was reduced, in his unfortunate expedition againft Naples, he difpatched the Seigneur de Craon into France, to procure a fupply of money; but this nobleman, after having raifed a confiderable fum, inftead of carrying it to his mafter, fquandered it at Venice in entertainments

KINGS OF FRANCE, &c. 21

tertainments and courtezans. On his return to Paris, the duke of Berri accufed him as the author of his brother's death; and having afterwards committed an affaffination in the ftreets, he was obliged to take fhelter in Bretagne, where the duke received and protected him. Charles, inftigated by his minifters, demanded the criminal, and on the duke's refufal, prepared to feize him by force; he fet out in perfon at the head of a confiderable army: as he continued his march through a foreft between Mans and La Fleche, in the daytime, a tall man, black and hideous, came from among the trees, and feizing his horfe's bridle, cried out, "Arrete Roi! ou " vas tu? Tu es trahi."——then difappeared. The king however purfued his journey, in defiance of this denunciation, when a fecond accident, purely cafual, produced on him effects the moft violent and unhappy.—It was in the month of Auguft, and the heats were infupportable. A page who carried the king's lance, being fallen afleep on his horfe, let it fall upon a helmet

met which another bore before him ; the noife which this caufed, the fight of the lance, and the words of the phantom recurring all at once to the king's imagination, he thought they were going to deliver him to his enemies, and this apprehenfion acting ftrongly on his fenfes, produced an inftant fit of madnefs. He drew his fword, and ftriking furioufly at all thofe about him, killed and wounded feveral, before any one had force or addrefs enough to feize him: they effected it at laft; the king fpent with his efforts, fell into a fort of lethargic fwoon, and in this condition they carried him, tied down, in a cart, to the city of Mans.

The ftory of the man in the wood appears at firft fight fo apparently fictitious, that one fhould certainly be induced to treat it as fuch, if, fuperadded to the univerfal teftimony of the cotemporary writers, fome of them did not give us reafon to believe, that the duke of Burgundy fet on foot this engine. He was the ftrict ally of the duke of Bretagne; he had ftrongly oppofed

oppofed the king's march; he was become unneceffary and powerlefs. Charles had only juft recovered from a fever at Amiens, in which he had given fome fymptoms of a difordered underftanding, which the phantom and fright were extremely calculated, in that fuperftitious and barbarous age, to heighten into frenzy.

The miferable prince recovered his fenfes on the third day, but not that clearnefs of perception and underftanding which he had previoufly enjoyed; and the expedition being rendered abortive, he was carried back to Paris by his uncles.

The incapacity of the king for public affairs reduced him once more to a ftate of tutelage; and the neceffity of vefting the regal power in more able hands, brought into light on this occafion two characters which hitherto lay in a fort of obfcurity——I mean the queen, and the duke of Orleans. The firft of thefe, Ifabella of Bavaria, was a princefs of uncommon perfonal beauty: fond of pleafure, to which fhe facrificed without reftraint, ſtraint, her thirſt of power was not leſs infatiable: of captivating addreſs, ſhe excelled in the arts of intrigue. Violent, vindictive, and capable of actions the moſt ſavage and unnatural in the purſuit of her favourite objects, ſhe involved the kingdom in war and tumult; violated the firſt feelings of a parent, by diſinheriting her offspring; and lived to become ſupremely odious and deſpicable, even to that party for whom ſhe had ſacrificed every confideration of honour or humanity.

The duke of Orleans was the only brother of the king: he had juſt attained his twentieth year, when the event which I have related placed him in a ſituation to pretend to the poſſeſſion of the firſt office under the crown. If his unripe youth ſeemed to diſqualify him for ſo high and important a truſt, his proximity of blood approached him by one degree nearer to the throne than his competitor the duke of Burgundy. His character reſembled in many reſpects that of his uncle the duke of Anjou, late regent. The ſame rapacity:

KINGS OF FRANCE, &c. 25

city: equal or greater profusion: more impetuous passions. Amorous from complexion, and formed by nature to succeed in gallantry, he set no bounds, he drew no veil before his excesses. Though married very early to Valentina of Milan, a princess of genius, beauty and accomplishments, and who was most tenderly attached to him, he indulged himself in all the libertinism of debauchery, and after the madness of his brother, entered into connections with the queen, which there is every reason to suppose were criminal and incestuous. His ambition was however disappointed for the present; and the states, being assembled in this critical emergency, conferred the administration of affairs on the duke of Burgundy.——Meanwhile the wretched king recovered in some degree his health and intellects, when another accident, scarce less extraordinary than those which first deprived him of them, again produced a fatal relapse. As it shews the nature of the diversions of the court in that uncultivated age, I shall relate it.

At

At a ball which was given in honour of the marriage of one of the queen's attendants, the king danced; a band of mafques entered the apartment, linked together with chains, and habited as bears. The duke of Orleans, willing to regard them clofely, took a flambeau in his hand, and holding it too near, unhappily fet fire to their habits, which being covered with pitch were inftantly in a blaze: three of them were burned to death: the room was all in flames; every one anxious for their own prefervation forgot the king, and he was on the point of being involved in this difmal cataftrophe, when the duchefs of Berri, with infinite prefence of mind, wrapt him in her manteau, and preferved him from the danger.—This rude fhock produced a fecond accefs of frenzy, and, as the ideas of magic and forcery were univerfally received in thofe times, the people imputed it to charms and incantations. After all the arts of medicine then known were exhaufted, recourfe was had to magicians, proceffions, and fafts——but the malady was

was incurable, and accompanied the unhappy monarch, though with intervals of reafon, to the tomb.

The government during the fucceeding years prefents a frightful picture. The difcordant interefts and contending parties of the two dukes of Orleans and Burgundy, grew up into factions of the moft rancorous and inveterate animofity. The people were loaded with exactions the moft oppreffive. Order, œconomy, public glory, and internal tranquillity had fled from France. The wife laws and falutary edicts of Charles the fifth were obliterated, or counteracted, and the kingdom, involved in calamity, was only preferved from a renewal of the Englifh invafions by fimilar evils, which prevented and retarded them.

In his intervals of recovery, Charles was carried as a pageant to fpectacles of ftate; he met the Englifh prince (Richard the fecond) near Calais, where they formed an unnatural alliance between this latter and Ifabella, daughter to Charles, only feven years of age, and which was never confummated,

fummated. A year or two afterwards, he was brought to Rheims, to receive Wenceflaus the emperor. That brutal and defpicable monarch, whom his fubjects, weary of his exceffes, juftly depofed, amid the fplendor of his reception, gave proofs of a fubjection to his appetites the moft unreftrained and debafed. When the dukes of Berri and Bourbon came in the morning to carry him to a banquet, to which the king had previoufly invited him, they found him vomiting the wine he had drank, and incapacitated by drunkennefs for the entertainment *.

* Thefe vifits of fovereign princes to each other, were common in that age. Charles the fourth, emperor of Germany, made one to Charles the fifth of France, at Paris, and was magnificently received.— Wenceflaus being totally incapable, from drunkennefs, of waiting on the king, was regaled by him the following day, when he exerted the greateft effort of reftraint and felf-denial over his appetites, in not intoxicating himfelf before dinner. The feftivities and debaucheries of the two monarchs rekindled Charles's madnefs, and neceffitated him to break up the interview, and return to the capital.

When

KINGS OF FRANCE, &c. 29

When Charles relapfed into madnefs * he was violent and untractable : he could not fupport the queen's prefence, and often proceeded even to ftrike her. Valentina duchefs of Orleans alone was acceptable to

* The picture which Jean Juvenal des Urfins, (a cotemporary writer of great credit,) has given of the king's unhappy malady, is fo fimple and touching, that I cannot difpenfe with inferting it. It will excite commiferation very highly.

" C'étoit grande pitié de la maladie du Roi, et ne
" connoiſſoit perfonne quélconque. Lui-même fe de-
" connoiſſoit, et difoit que ce n'étoit il pas. On
" lui amenoit la Reine, et fembloit qu'il ne l'eut onc-
" ques vue; et n'en avoit point memoire, ne con-
" noiſſance, ne d'hommes ou de femmes quelconques,
" excepté de la ducheſſe d'Orleans; car il la voyoit
" et regardoit très volontiers, et l'appelloit belle fœur.
" Et comme fouvent il y a de mauvaifes langues, on
" difoit, et publioient aucuns, qu'elle l'avoit enfor-
" celé par le moyen de fon Pere le duc de Milan, qui
" étoit Lombard, et que en fon pays on ufoit de telles
" chofes ; et l'une de plus dolentes et couroucées
" qui y fut, c'étoit la ducheſſe d'Orleans, et n'eſt à
" croire ou prefumer qu'elle eut voulu faire ou
" penfer."

It appears by this account, with what contempt he treated the popular prejudices againſt the duchefs of Orleans.

him;

him; and as her appearance always calmed his agitations, and produced on him thofe effects, of which even lunatics are fufceptible towards an object beloved, fhe became deteftable to the people; who imputed all thefe fymptoms and changes to magical powers, which fhe was fuppofed to have ufed to deftroy the king.—The adminiftration mean while fluctuated between the rival factions: that of Orleans gained a fhort afcendant, which was abufed to fuch fevere oppreffion, that the Burgundian party regained the fuperiority; when the king emerging from one of his long fits of infanity, and influenced by the cries of his people, deprived both the dukes of all authority, which he principally vefted in the queen and council.

The two factions, confirmed by perpetual competition, were tranfmitted to fucceeding generations. Philip duke of Burgundy died in Brabant, and his fon John, furnamed " Sans Peur," fucceeded to his ample territories, to his place and pretenfions. He had all that magnificence and princely

princely splendor in his character which so peculiarly distinguished the house of Burgundy, and seemed hereditary in the line. His intrepidity and love of power were not inferior to his munificence; and the turbulent chaos of government in the court, soon gave him an opportunity to renew the scenes which had been acted under his father.

Charles, relapsed again into the horrors of his former condition, could oppose no barrier to the oppressions or malversations of those who possessed themselves of his authority. Isabella and the duke of Orleans had entered into connections of the most intimate nature, and divided between them the regal power. The clamours of the Parisians, scandalized at an union so apparently personal and unjustifiable, and driven to despair by the unprecedented rapacity exercised over them, recalled the Burgundian, and he was received with acclamations. He took his seat in the council: the queen and duke retired to Melun, and left the field to their competitor.

John neglected not the occasion to confirm his influence.—He affianced his daughter to the young dauphin Louis: he affected an attention to the unhappy king, whom his wife and brother had shamefully abandoned to want and naftinefs during his fits*. He gained the people by an alleviation of the imposts: and a mock reconciliation at laft took place, on which the queen returned to Paris, and the two dukes embracing, heard mafs together, and fwore on the facra-

---

* Juvenal des Urfins draws a frightful and almoft incredible picture of Charles the fixth's miferable condition in his acceffes of frenzy. The governante of the royal children avowed to him in one of his lucid intervals, that fhe frequently had not wherewithal to feed or cloath them.—" Alas!" anfwered the king, with a figh, " I am myfelf no better treated."—' He held in his hand a golden cup, in which he had juft drank, and this he gave to her for the fupply of his children's neceffities.

ments

ments an eternal oblivion of paſt animoſities.

Thoſe who know human nature well, will not be ſurpriſed to find the duke of Orleans's aſſaſſination following almoſt immediately theſe marks of diſſembled friendſhip. He was returning from the hotel de St. Pol, where he had ſpent the evening with Iſabella, who was newly recovered from a lying-in. The duke rode on a mule, accompanied only by two or three valets : it was night : a Norman gentleman, whom revenge for the loſs of a poſt of which he had deprived him, ſtimulated to the attempt, ſurrounded him with eighteen aſſaſſins in the " rue Barbette." He cut off his hand with the firſt blow of a battle-ax : at the ſecond, he tumbled him from his mule; and with the third, he opened his ſcull, leaving him dead on the ground. All the troop then made their eſcape, and took refuge in the duke of Burgundy's palace.

The motives to this deteſtable crime are ſomewhat ambiguous and obſcure : the French

French hiftorians fay they were more perfonal than political. The gallantries of the duke of Orleans were notorious; and it is pretended, that he had not only profited of the duchefs of Burgundy's favours, but had even the temerity and infolence to brave the unfortunate hufband, by introducing him into a cabinet hung with the portraits of thofe women he had enjoyed, among which his own wife held a diftinguifhed place *. To whatever
caufe

---

* Duhaillan affigns this amour as the caufe of his murder; and Brantome confirms it as the tradition of his time. Thefe are his words:

" Louis duc d'Orleans, aieul de Louis douze,
" s'étant vanté tout haut dans un banquet ou étoit
" le duc Jean de Bourgogne fon coufin, qu'il avoit
" en fon cabinet les portraits des plus belles dames
" dont il avoit joui; par cas fortuit, un jour le duc
" Jean entrant dans ce cabinet, la premiere dame
" qu'il vit pourtraite, et fe prefenta du premier afpect
" devant fes yeux, ce fut fa noble dame et époufe,
" qu'on tenoit de ce temps très belle."

Yet Olivier de la Marche in his Memoirs declares, that the duke of Burgundy, too credulous, haftily believed an information given him, that Louis duke
of

KINGS OF FRANCE, &c. 35

cause it be ascribed, the kingdom long felt its pernicious consequences, and the perpetrator met with an exact retribution

of Orleans had plotted to assassinate him, and resolving to anticipate the blow, caused him to be put to death. On that night he had spent part of the evening with Isabella. About seven o'clock, one of the king's valets de chambre came to inform the duke, that his majesty wished to see him immediately on an affair of importance: he went out, accompanied only by two gentlemen, and some footmen who carried flambeaux. The Norman gentleman's name, who headed the band, and dispatched him, was Raoullet Ocquetouville: he had been one of the duke's retainers; and Louis having caused his name to be erased from the list of the officers of his household, he determined on vengeance. The assassins, to elude pursuit, set on fire a neighbouring house, and scattered gins or traps in the streets. The duke of Burgundy affected at first the utmost sorrow for his cousin's death; he attended his funerals, lamented and wept for him—but when it was resolved in council to search the houses of all the princes and nobles, to discover the murderers, he was so troubled and terrified that he took the duke of Bourbon aside, and confessed to him that he was himself the author of the crime. The ensuing day he fled into Flanders with his assassins. These are the chief and most interesting particulars of that atrocious murder.

many years afterwards on the bridge of Montereau.

To give a picture of the reign of Charles the fixth, from this æra to the battle of Azincourt, is to enumerate a feries of profcriptions, maffacres, and barbarities almoft unparalleled in any century. Marius or Sylla never exercifed more unrelenting vengeance over their vanquifhed enemies in ancient Rome, than did the Armagnacs and Burgundians, as they triumphed by turns in Paris. Two thoufand citizens perifhed in one carnage.

The young duke of Orleans, only fixteen years old, fucceeded to his father's place, and loudly demanded vengeance for his murder. Valentina, his mother, died of grief and difappointed revenge, in the flower of her age. Ifabella, deprived of her lover and her faithful partizan, retired from Paris overcome with terror—while the duke of Burgundy, too powerful to be amenable to punifhment, not only avowed his crime, but even attempted to excufe and juftify it. The court, the ca-
capital,

KINGS OF FRANCE, &c. 37

pital, the kingdom, and the perſon of the ſovereign, were alternately ſeized on by the oppoſite leaders. Anarchy and uproar, and all the ſcourges of public diſcord, lorded it unrepreſſed and unreſtrained.

The young dauphin, Louis, began to appear amid this ſcene of confuſion; but his character, fickle, inconſtant, diſſolute, and graſping at unlimited power, rather increaſed than repreſſed the accumulated evils of ſtate.

The king, as he regained from time to time ſome faint gleams of reaſon, was rendered ſubſervient to every purpoſe of the predominant faction; and was now the protector, and now the avenger of the duke of Burgundy. During his returns of inſanity, he was often indecently neglected, without table, without neceſſary finances, even almoſt without changes of habit. As he was generally obſtinate likewiſe, and difficult to manage at theſe times, a young and beautiful miſtreſs was procured for him, of whom he became enamoured, as he had been of the ducheſs Valentina,

Valentina, and who alone had any influence or command over him *.

Paris, long oppreſſed, became ſeditious; and as it had ſuffered ſo ſeverely from the abuſe of the royal power, attempted to repreſs and reduce it to narrower bounds. Such was the deplorable condition of the kingdom, when the ſtorm which had long menaced, and which had been pro-

* Odette de Champdivers was daughter to a dealer in horſes: ſhe was young, lively, and beautiful. The queen herſelf firſt preſented her to Charles the ſixth: he was preſently enamoured of this new miſtreſs. Her authority over him was ſo great, in his fits of frenzy, that ſhe obtained the name of " La " Petite Reine;" under which title ſhe is commonly known in hiſtory. The unhappy king, when ſeized with madneſs, would often perſiſt to keep the ſame linen or ſheets, how dirty ſoever; nor could any perſon except Odette induce him to defiſt from this reſolution. Charles cohabited with her, and even had by her a daughter named Margaret de Valois. Charles the ſeventh acknowledged her as his ſiſter, gave her a very ample portion, and married her to the Seigneur de Belleville in Poictou. Claude, the laſt of their deſcendants, was killed in the battle of Coutras, in 1587.

tracted

tracted by a chain of incidents, burſt at length.——Henry the fourth of England, who held his uſurpation by a tenure too precarious to engage in foreign wars, was dead; and a young prince to whom the crown deſcended by a ſort of hereditary preſcription, and gifted with all the qualities of a warrior and a general, ſaw and improved the opportunity. He revived the antiquated and ill-founded pretenſions of Edward to the crown of France: he landed in Normandy; and by the headſtrong impatience of his enemies, renewed at Azincourt the laurels won by his anceſtors under Philip and John. He retired into England, carrying with him the captive princes of the blood.

Conſternation and affright were ſuperadded to all the other convulſions of ſtate; and every calamity was heightened by this foreign invaſion.—At this juncture the dauphin Louis died. He promiſed no marks of happier times, nor can his death be regarded as a loſs to the kingdom. A dyſentery, occaſioned by his irregularities, probably carried him off, though poiſon was fufpected and pretended. His fecond brother, John, fucceeded to his rights.

This prince had been married to the duke of Burgundy's daughter, and was a zealous partizan of the faction; and as he too died within a year after the firft dauphin, it has been with more reafon fuppofed that violent and unnatural means were ufed for that purpofe. The ftory of his mother Ifabella having deftroyed him by a poifoned chain of gold which fhe fent him, is evidently falfe—but it is not equally clear, that Louis duke of Anjou, and king of Sicily, fon to the regent who perifhed in Calabria, was not the author of his death. This prince had married his daughter to Charles duke of Touraine, youngeft of the king's fons, and who afterwards mounted the throne; and it is faid, that to facilitate the acceffion of his fon-in-law, he had not fcrupled to remove both the elder brothers, who ftood between him and the crown *.

Charles,

* Mezerai feems to declare Louis the firft dauphin poifoned. " Il tomba malade," fays he, " d'un
" flux

Charles, born to reinſtate the monarchy, attacked on every ſide, had been educated in ſentiments of the utmoſt deteſtation for the duke of Burgundy, and of attachment to the houſe of Orleans. The queen his mother, who had now united her intereſt with the former, was therefore ſent by his approval and permiſſion under a guard to Tours, after he had executed a ſingular vengeance on one of her lovers, named Louis Bois-Bourdon; who was tied up in a ſack, and precipitated into the Seine, with this label annexed, " Laiſſez paſſer " la juſtice du roi !"—An outrage which

" flux de ventre, dont il mourut, non ſans des marques " apparentes de poiſon."—But he does not mention the perpetrators of this crime. It ſeems to be a fact much more univerſally eſtabliſhed, that John, duke of Touraine, ſecond dauphin, was put to death by unnatural means. Whether the king of Sicily was the author of it, can by no means be aſcertained; but his ambitious character juſtified the ſuſpicion. Even the duke of Burgundy was accuſed in the ſequel, but with much leſs reaſon or probability. He expired at the age of eighteen, at Compiegne in Picardy.

Iſabella

Ifabella never pardoned him, and which fhe feverely revenged!

The queen's imprifonment was of fhort duration: fhe was refcued by the duke of Burgundy, and affumed the regency. It is pretended that fhe had not lefs complaifance for the murderer of the duke of Orleans, than fhe had fhewn to the duke himfelf; nor is there any difficulty in believing, that a princefs ever a flave to paffions the moft impetuous, and whofe irregularity of manners was notorious, did not hefitate to gratify her protector and deliverer by every compliance with his wifhes. Her age, which was about forty-fix or forty-feven years at this time, forms no objection; fince fhe is univerfally allowed to have poffeffed a beauty the moft captivating and perfect *.

Mean-

---

* The cotemporary writers in general accufe the duke of Burgundy of criminal connections with the queen. He carried her off from the church of Marmoutier near Tours, and conducted her to Chartres. Pontus Heuterus, in his life of John, exprefsly mentions

Meanwhile Henry the fifth landing again in Normandy, reduced all that fertile province under his fubjection, unoppofed by any enemy. The Burgundian party, once more triumphant, re-entered the capital in all the fplendor of conqueft; and took a vengeance the moft fanguinary on their opponents. The wretched king remained in their poffeffion, and fcarce was the dauphin faved by Tannegui du Chaftel. The Englifh monarch, at the head of a victorious army, approached. He demanded Catherine of France, and the fucceffion to the kingdom, with the immediate inveftiture of the regency under his father-in-law. Ifabella, defperate, unnatural, deftitute of every fentiment of a mother or a queen, hefitated not to execute thefe ignominious and

tions Ifabella as *one* of his miftreffes. Thefe are his words—" Mulierofior patre multo fuit; viva enim
" uxore, *pellices* non ignobiles habuit, quorum facile
" princeps extremis vitæ temporibus, Giaci fuit do-
" mina (de Giac) *ipfaque regis Caroli fexti uxor*, non
" fatis bene audivit."

haughty

haughty demands. She even carried her daughter to Troyes with that intention—but the Burgundian prince, fprung from the blood of France; nor yet loft to the feelings of patriotifm, of duty, and of public glory, paufed at this fatal ftep. He faw its almoft certain and irremediable confequences : he determined to fruftrate them e're too late. An accommodation with the dauphin might yet retrieve the falling ftate; Charles invited and implored him to it : Every principle of virtue demanded it.

An interview was agreed on at the bridge of Montereau-fur-Yonne; in this, a total amnefty of paft crimes, murders, and animofities was to take place on both fides, and a coalition of arms and interefts to fucceed.—But whether the duke dreaded the vengeance of his coufin's death; or whether he fufpected the dauphin's fincerity, he did not come to the place of rendezvous till after he had been waited for fifteen days. It is faid his miftrefs, the lady of Gyac, by an ungenerous treachery, perfuaded

perfuaded him at length to venture. Every precaution was taken to infure his fafety: a barrier was erected on the bridge; he placed his guard at one end, and advancing with ten attendants, threw himfelf on his knees before the dauphin. At that inftant Tannegui du Chaftel making the fignal, leaped the barrier with fome others, and giving him the firft blow, he was almoft immediately difpatched. Though Charles was only a paffive fpectator of this affaffination, yet it cannot be doubted that he was privy to its commiffion; nor does his unripe age, though it may palliate, exculpate him from the infamy of fuch a participation, fince he continued his protection and favour to its perpetrators *.

Never

* There is a certain veil of uncertainty and darknefs drawn over this foul tranfaction. The partizans of Charles the feventh pretend, that John had intended to execute as bloody and perfidious a vengeance on him at the bridge of Montereau, as he had done on the duke of Orleans fome years before at Paris: But there is little probability in this affertion. Juvenal

des

Never was any action more fatal to France. Ifabella, loud in her exclamations, and bent on the deftruction of her fon, called for immediate vengeance.—Philip, who fucceeded his father in the dukedom of Burgundy, was compelled to efpoufe her caufe by every principle of filial piety and juft refentment. They refolved on a marriage between Catherine, and the Eng-

---

dès Urfins exprefsly fays, " Que la dame de Giac, " maitreffe du duc, fut celle qui le determina à fe " trouver à cette entrevue." If the folicitations of his miftrefs were requifite to induce him to go to the interview, it is not poffible to fufpect him of a premeditated defign to murder the dauphin. Tannegui du Chaftel, and John Louvet prefident of Provence, were the duke's inveterate and mortal enemies. To delude him more perfectly, the caftle of Montereau was delivered into his poffeffion, but deftitute either of provifions or engines of defence. The duke came down on the bridge with ten attendants. In the pofture he was, on his knees, it was not difficult to difpatch him. Of the perfons who accompanied him, only Archembaud de Foix, Seigneur de Noailles, attempted to defend his lord. He perifhed with him at the fame moment. It feems impoffible to acquit Charles of a participation in this crime.

lish monarch. It was solemnized at Troyes; and she brought the kingdom in dowry to her husband.

By an unexampled and astonishing concurrence of circumstances, a foreign prince was on the point of being seated in the throne of France. The dauphin, unable to resist so powerful a combination, retired southward, and began to fortify himself in the provinces beyond the Loire. Henry was proclaimed regent, and even took upon him the exercise of the regal power, which the maladies of Charles incapacitated him to use. The defeat and death of his brother, the duke of Clarence, at Baugé in Anjou, only protracted for a moment the destruction of the dauphin. The English prince returning from his own kingdom, prepared to push him to the last extremities: he was declared guilty of the duke of Burgundy's murder, summoned to a solemn trial, and disinherited from the succession.

Henry himself began his march from Paris, armed with the united forces of France

France and Burgundy.—The moment approached of young Charles's inevitable ruin——when by one of thofe extraordinary incidents which decide the fate of nations, Henry, the fortunate and the victorious, expired in the flower of youth. As far as human forefight can determine from appearances; had he lived—or even had the fucceffion defcended to his brother the duke of Bedford—the family of Valois would have been overwhelmed by fuch a multiplicity of concomitant evils, and an Englifh ufurper eftablifhed his authority over France.——But by his death the miferable kingdom had time to recover. An infant at the breaft fucceeded to the two crowns; and the dauphin, re-afcending by flow degrees the hill of fortune, reftored his declining affairs.

The death of Henry the fifth was wondroufly critical. The miferable Charles, his father-in-law, furvived him only fix-and-fifty days. He breathed his laft in the hotel de St. Pol at Paris, attended in his dying moments by a fingle gentleman of the

the bed-chamber, a confeffor, and an almoner. No funeral honours were paid him; no prince of the blood attended his proceffion; and the abandoned wretchednefs which marked almoft his whole life, attended him to the tomb where he was depofited.

Here let us paufe a moment! A mind philofophic and reflective, which views with equal and impartial eye the changes of human affairs, and revolutions of empires;—which regards all thofe effects or phænomena, imputed by the multitude to fupernatural and extraordinary interpofitions, as regularly flowing from fixed and ftated caufes;—which, comprehenfive in its furvey, enlarged in its conceptions, forms a juft and folid eftimate of things: —fuch a fpectator will find, at this remarkable æra of the French monarchy, ample field for fpeculation; and will allow the juftice of that obfervation of the Tacitus of the eighteenth century,

tury, " That there is in all governments an
" ultimate point of depreſſion and of ele-
" vation, at which affairs revert, and re-
" turn in a contrary direction.

CHAPTER THE SECOND.

Political condition of France.—Character of John duke of Bedford.—Accession and distresses of Charles the seventh.—Appearance of the maid of Orleans.—Character of Agnes Soreille.—Deaths of the queen dowager, and duke of Bedford.—Louis the dauphin's treasonable practices, and flight.—Death of Agnes Soreille.—Circumstances of it.—English ultimately driven out of France.—Dauphin's disobedience,—Oppressions, and retreat into Burgundy.—Charles's fruitless attempts to gain possession of his person.—The king's illness.—Death.—Character.

THERE is perhaps no point of time in the history of France more interesting to an English reader, than that where the last chapter concluded. The death of Henry the fifth, arrested in the very moment when he prepared to overwhelm

whelm the dauphin; and that of Charles the fixth, by which the crown devolved to his fon; feemed to be events fo important, and big with confequences, that a change the moft fudden and rapid was to be expected from them.—But though the former of thefe incidents left the reduction of France incomplete and unfinifhed, it did not abfolutely render it abortive. In John duke of Bedford, left regent of the two kingdoms, furvived the fpirit of his brother Henry. Even the colours under which he is depictured to us by the French hiftorians, figure a prince worthy of the great truft repofed in him, and capable of all the toils of empire. He had juft attained the prime of manhood; nor could the tutelage of his infant nephew, who was ftill at the breaft, have been configned to more virtuous and able hands. Ifabella, the declared enemy of her fon; and Philip duke of Burgundy, reduced by a fatal neceffity to turn his arms againft the protector of his father's murderers, encreafed his power:

all

all the northern provinces, and Guyenne, were already reduced under fubjection.

Charles, on the other hand, retired into the fortreffes of the Cevennes, or the mountains of Auvergne; not yet arrived to years of majority, and only attended by fome princes of the blood, and a few brave adventurers animated by confiderations of loyalty and love to their expiring country, could only make a feeble oppofition to fuch powerful enemies. On the news of his father's death, he was faluted king by his little band of adherents, and even crowned at Poitiers *; but to fo extreme penury was he reduced, that even the affectionate fidelity of his queen, who fold all her plate and jewels for his fubfift-

* The dauphin Charles, fays Mezerai, was at the caftle d'Efpailly, near Puy, in Auvergne, when he received the news of his father's death. On the firft day he wore mourning: the enfuing one, he dreffed himfelf in fcarlet, and after having heard mafs, he ordered the banner of France to be elevated in the chapel. The nobles who adhered to him, then faluted him fovereign, with loud acclamations of " Vive le roi !"

ance,

ance, scarce sufficed to provide for the immediate wants of his dress and table; and he was driven to distresses only equalled by those which Mary of Medicis, and Henrietta queen of England underwent during their exile in the last century.

During the first six years of his reign, the English arms were almost uniformly triumphant; and though he gained over to his party the celebrated Arthur count de Richemont, brother to the duke of Bretagne; yet this imperious chieftain, rough and ferocious in his manners, treated his sovereign with the most mortifying indignity; and unsheathed the sword of constable, not only against his opponents, but against his dearest favourites, whom he stabbed or drowned even in the royal presence *.

The

---

* The constable first compelled the king to renounce and banish Louvet, and Tannegui du Chastel, to both of whom he was most warmly attached. The Seigneur de Gyac, who succeeded to their place in Charles's favour and affections, he seized by force

at

The little court of Charles was torn by inteftine factions; and he would doubtlefs have been himfelf the victim of fo many calamities, if fimilar or fiercer diffentions had not arifen between the two dukes of Burgundy and Glocefter, on the fubject of the beautiful Jacqueline countefs of Hainault. In vain did Bedford, animated only by motives of the moft patriotic and glorious nature, implore his brother to defift from his unjuft pretenfions. In vain did he reprefent to him the interefts of their common prince and nephew; and point out to him that the moment was arrived to extinguifh for ever the race of Valois.—Glocefter was

at Iffoudun in Berri, while in bed, and after fome fhort forms of pretended juftice, caufed him to be drowned.—Only a few months afterwards, he executed a fimilar vengeance on the Camus de Beaulieu, another gentleman obnoxious to his difpleafure, and acceptable to the king. The court was at Poitiers; and the marechal de Bouffac, by order of the count de Richemont, killed the unhappy favourite in the ftreet, and almoft under his mafter's eye.

deaf

deaf to his entreaties or expoſtulations; and that precife juncture in the affairs of human life, which if paſſed, rarely or never returns, was irrecoverably loſt. The regent, notwithſtanding, though almoſt unſupported by his allies, maintained the war: he found reſources in his own character, in his popularity, his affability, his munificence, and clemency of adminiſtration, which had attached to him even the Pariſians.

The Engliſh were animated by a long train of ſucceſs, commanded by experienced leaders, and oppoſed to troops diſpirited and ſinking under adverſe fortune. The memorable ſiege of Orleans was undertaken. Though Dunois, the immortal baſtard of Orleans, exerted every effort of valour and conduct againſt the beſiegers, it was vigorouſly preſſed. Charles already began to meditate a retreat into Dauphiné, and all ſeemed to conſpire for his deſtruction; when an occurrence the moſt ſingular in the records of hiſtory, turned the current in his favour, and reſtored

ſtored him to the throne of his anceſtors.
—I mean the appearance of Joan d'Arc.
A village girl, either inſtigated by an en-
thuſiaſtic apprehenſion of ſupernatural
aſſiſtance, or inſtructed to feign ſuch a
belief, quits her obſcurity in Lorraine,
and goes to find the king at Chinon.

However we may ſuppoſe Joan herſelf
to have been perſuaded of her divine miſ-
ſion, it is ſcarce poſſible to imagine that
Charles and his courtiers accepted her
offers from any other motive, than that
of trying an extraordinary and deſperate
remedy, in the preſent diſorders of the
ſtate. The age was ignorant, credulous,
barbarous, and ſuperſtitious to a high
degree : it was exactly adapted to their
apprehenſions and religious terrors;
and while the count de Dunois really
commanded, Joan, unfurling the ſacred
ſtandard, headed the troops choſen to
ſuccour the city. It ſucceeded even beyond expectation. Like another Gideon,
armed with ethereal protection, ſhe attacked

tacked enemies already difmayed with fears, and obtained an eafy conqueft.

Not content with raifing the fiege of Orleans, and animated by the fortunate iffue of her firft effay in arms, fhe pufhed her views to the greateft length. One combat prepared the way for a fecond; and ftill advancing through provinces which had been totally in the power of the Englifh, fhe led her royal votary to Rheims, and faw him folemnly inaugurated.

The perfidy, or the imprudence of the governor of Compeigne, delivered her at length into the hands of her adverfaries. Even then fhe behaved, though defencelefs, and menaced with death, in a manner becoming a heroine. Her enthufiafm and reliance on fuperior aid fupported her courage—for Charles, who had derived all thofe benefits he wanted from fuch an engine, made no effort to procure her releafe; and a barbarous refentment, unworthy and unbecoming generous minds, prompted the Englifh, who had

fuffered

suffered so severely from her prowess, to take a cruel and inhuman revenge.

Meanwhile, though the duke of Bedford, in the hope of re-animating his depressed countrymen, caused young Henry to be crowned at Paris, the war languished on both sides, from their incapacity of exerting fresh efforts. Charles, naturally voluptuous, fond of pleasures, and a slave to beauty, had gladly quitted the fatigues of a camp to indulge his softer passions. His heart, susceptible of love, had found an object supremely capable of exciting it, in the celebrated Agnes Soreille. She was born at the village of Fromenteau, near Loches, in Touraine. Her personal attractions, which are represented by all the cotemporary historians, as the most touching and seductive, were equalled by the delicacy and gaiety of her imagination. She was worthy the lover she possessed, because, during all the unlimited influence which her charms procured her over him, she never forgot he was a king, nor sacrificed his glory and interests to the effeminate gratifications of appetite.

appetite. On the contrary, when immerſed in indolent and ſupine inaction, ſhe is ſaid to have rouſed him from his lethargy, and excited him to atchievements worthy his birth and dignity *.

The treaty concluded at Arras between

* The year of her birth was about 1409. She had attained her twenty-ſecond year when ſhe firſt appeared at court, in the ſervice of Iſabella queen of Naples and Sicily. From that princeſs ſhe paſſed into the train of Mary, Charles's queen. Her favour was during ſome time cloſely concealed, and only divulged by the promotion of all her relations to offices and dignities, " Acceſſit ad ſtupri ſuſpicionem propin-
" quorum Agnetis ad dignitates eccleſiaſticas repen-
" tina promotio," ſays Gaguin, in his life of Charles the ſeventh.

Her mind was elevated and noble. She ever attempted to inſpire the king with a thirſt of glory, and a wiſh to recover his dominions from the Engliſh. Francis the firſt honoured and cheriſhed her memory. The four elegant lines which that great prince made on her, are well known.

" Gentille Agnes, plus d'honneur tu merite,
" La cauſe étant de France recouvrer !
" Que ce que peut dans un cloitre ouvrer
" Clauſe Nonain, ou bien devote hermité."

Charles

KINGS OF FRANCE, &c. 61

Charles and the duke of Burgundy, who had long fluctuated in uncertainty, and yielded at length to sentiments of generous forgiveness, was a mortal wound to the English affairs. Isabella, who had been long an object of infamy and public detestation, expired of sorrow and consternation at this unwelcome news *; and the

* Isabella of Bavaria, one of the worst queens who has reigned in France, survived the unhappy Charles the sixth, her husband, about thirteen years. John Boucher, a writer not far removed from the time in which she lived, relates her death very minutely in his Annales d' Aquitaine.—— " Incontinent après le
" traité d'Arras (says he) Madame Yfabeau de Ba-
" viere, veuve du feu roi Charles 6, qui avoit été
" longuement entre les mains des Anglois en grande
" indigence et pauvreté, fut averti du dit accord et
" appointment, et en mourut de douleur en l'hotel du
" roi, près St. Paul à Paris ; et fut fon corps mené à
" St. Denis, et enterré en la chapelle des rois, près
" du feu Charles 6 fon mari. Elle n'eut que qua-
" tres cierges, et quatres perfonnes à fon enterrement.
" Ce fut grand' honte aux Anglois, qui l'avoient en
" leurs mains, qu'ils ne lui firent aucun honneur à
" fes exeques."

Her fon, Charles the feventh, being born at the time

the regent, whofe mafterly and judicious policy had alone hitherto preferved the declining affairs of his country, in that fwift decay to which they apparently haftened, followed foon after.

The Parifians received their native prince into his capital with acclamations; and Charles, after long oppofing a fea of

---

time when her intimacy with Louis duke of Orleans was carried to the greatcft length, gave fome probability to the report that he was the offspring of their inceftuous amours. It is faid that even the Englifh, whom fhe had fo highly obliged, at the expence of honour, nature, and affection, were fo ungenerous as to reproach her with this humiliating circumftance. Mezerai fays, " Ils prenoient plaifir de lui dire en " face que le roi Charles n'étoit pas fils de fon mari." —Gaguin ufes nearly the fame words: " Nulla re " magis irritata, quam quod Carolum regem, ejus " filium incefto concubitu natum Anglus diffama- " bat."

Her funerals were meaner than thofe of an ordinary gentlewoman. Her body was carried in a little boat on the Seine to St. Denis, attended only by four perfons; and the prior of St. Denis performed the fervice, not a prelate being prefent, or any folemnities paid to her remains.

troubles,

troubles, began to tafte the pleafures of conqueft and tranquillity. The condition of France was, notwithftanding, at this period the moft deplorable and wretched. It prefented a renewal of the fad fcenes which had been exhibited under John, and in the firft years of Charles the fifth. A diforder in the provinces, approaching to anarchy.—The calamities of war were followed by the fcourge of peftilence and famine.—The foldiery, unemployed during the frequent truces which took place between the two crowns, ravaged the poffeffions of the defencelefs peafants. As yet the regal power was not fufficiently confirmed, to extend any permanent and effectual remedy to thefe evils; and as Charles appears principally to have refided in the royal chateaus on the Loire, or in Berri, Paris is faid to have been fo depopulated and abandoned, that the wolves ventured even into the middle of the "rue St. Antoine," and carried off the children of the citizens.——A circumftance, which if true,

indicates

indicates a state of the most dreadful and complete misery!

The passionate desire of redressing these national distresses, induced the king to hold out terms of pacification to the English, neither inglorious or disadvantageous. The two rich provinces of Normandy and Guyenne were offered them, under condition of homage. Sound policy should have induced and dictated a compliance with these cessions —— but Bedford was no more. Henry, the weakest prince who ever held a sceptre, meek and superstitious, was ill qualified to guide the helm of state, in conjunctures delicate and critical. The factions of Winchester and Glocester tore the court; and the nation, accustomed to triumph in every preceding contest with France, and still supported by the recollection of Henry's and Edward's trophies, knew not how to adopt a temporising and more humiliating tone. Though a suspension of arms was accepted for some years, they did not recede from
their

their ancient and ill-founded pretenſions on the kingdom.

Meanwhile France ſaw expire the inveterate animoſity and hereditary hatred of the two houſes of Burgundy and Orleans. The firſt of theſe princes, by an effort of magnanimity and greatneſs of ſoul rarely found among men; deſirous to bury in oblivion the unhappy diſſentions of his father, reſtored the duke of Orleans, who had languiſhed in a captivity of five-and-twenty years, ever ſince the battle of Azincourt, to liberty, by paying his ranſom, which amounted to the enormous ſum of three hundred thouſand ecus. They met at Gravelines, embraced, and interchanged a mutual forgiveneſs.

During the tranquillity of the peace, Charles, occupied in the purſuits of love, in banquets, gardens, and the pleaſures of the chace, indulged his natural inclination for theſe gentler recreations, and forgot the toils of war. The beautiful Agnes poſſeſſed an unlimited influence over him.—But deſtined, like his unhappy ſucceſſor,

successor, Henry the fourth, after having vanquished his foreign enemies, to find more cruel ones in his own household; fortune had prepared in his son a source of disquietude more sharp and afflictive than any external ones could prove. Louis, the detestable and malignant Louis, his eldest son, had already attained his twenty-second year, though the king was still in the vigour of his age. When only sixteen, he had rebelled against his father, who forgave his misconduct. Such lenity was lost on his obdurate and unfeeling mind. Discontented, and anxious to anticipate his power, he refused subjection, and proceeded to insults the most irritating and criminal.—An incident, which, as it peculiarly marks his character, I shall relate, happened at this time.

A person of the court had offended the dauphin: determined on revenge, he bargained with the count de Dammartin to assassinate him; but the count, being dissuaded from the perpetration of so mean and dastardly a crime by his brother, refused

refused to execute it. The affair came to the king's knowledge, who severely reprimanded his son. Louis, to cover his own guilt, accused the count of having suggested to him the means; but Dammartin, jealous of his wounded honour, not only denied the accusation in the royal presence; but offered, according to the laws of chivalry, to justify himself from the imputation, in single combat, against any of the dauphin's train. Charles, whose character was peculiarly open, generous, and candid, saw and abhorred the malignity of his son: he even ordered him to quit his presence, and not appear at court for four months. The dauphin obeyed, but not without menaces; and retired into Dauphiné, from whence he returned no more till the king's death.

The war between France and England, which had slumbered for several years, at length waked again; but conquest, which during the beginning of Charles's reign hung dubious, now declared uniformly in his favour. He attacked Normandy, undertook

undertook the fiege of Rouen in perfon, and re-entered it in triumph. The gallant count de Dunois feconded his fovereign's efforts, and in a few months the whole province was finally re-annexed to the crown, from which Henry the fifth had difmembered it.

The pleafure which Charles felt from this important and victorious campaign, was faddened by the lofs of his beloved miftrefs. She expired of a dyfentery, at the abbey of Jumieges, near Rouen; to which place fhe had come to meet the king, and to inform him of a confpiracy againft his perfon. Though the cotemporary authors exprefs themfelves with a ftudied ambiguity on this event, there is great reafon to believe that the dauphin was concerned in the plot; and even that Agnes's death was the effect of poifon adminiftered by his exprefs command. The king tenderly and paffionately lamented her: fhe was one of the beft and greateft miftreffes which any of the French princes have poffeffed. Madame de Villequier,

quier, her niece, by a fort of inheritance in gallantry, fucceeded to her place and favour *.

The reduction of Normandy was only a prelude to new acquifitions: the king, animated by his paft fuccefs, refolved to

* Agnes Soreille was created by Charles the feventh countefs of Penthievre, and lady of Beauté fur Marne. She was in her fortieth year when fhe died; and left three daughters by the king. Charlotte, the eldeft, was married to Jacques de Brezé, count de Maulevrier: her death was truly deplorable. She is faid to have equalled her mother in beauty; but an attachment which her hufband difcovered, proved her ruin. Jean de Troyes has related the circumftances of it: they are fo affecting that I fhall infert them without any alteration:—" Elle étoit allé à la chaffe
" avec lui; à leur retour chacun fe retiroit dans fon
" appartement; Brezé fut averti que fa femme s'étoit
" retirée avec Pierre de la Vergne, fon veneur: il
" prend fon epée, fait brifer la porte, trouve la
" Vergne en chemife, et le tue. Sa femme s'alla
" cacher fous la couverture d'un lit ou étoient
" couchés fes enfans. Il la tira du lit, et lui plongea
" fon épée dans le Sein: elle étoit à genoux; elle
" tomba morte."—Louis the eleventh obliged the count de Maulevrier to purchafe a remiffion of this crime, by an enormous pecuniary amende.

F 3 improve

improve the favourable moment, and to attempt what his grandfather's untimely and lamented death had then prevented— the entire rout of the Englifh, and their extirpation from his dominions. All Guienne and Gafcony was ftill in their poffeffion: the inhabitants, governed during feveral centuries by them, were affectionate to thefe foreign mafters; and a very vigorous defence might yet have been made—but civil and inteftine confufion aided Charles's arms. The bloody quarrel between the contending Rofes, which deluged the kingdom with flaughter, was already on the point of commencing. No fuccours were fent, no timely aid afforded them. Four armies, commanded by the ableft generals of France, entered thefe provinces, and made a progrefs the moft fortunate and rapid: only one effort was exerted for their prefervation by the great Talbot and his fon, who perifhed in the battle of Caftillon. Bourdeaux and Bayonne opened their gates to the conqueror; and Charles the feventh, who had acceded to the crown
under

under circumstances the most distressful and deplorable, yet effected what neither the policy or courage of his ancestors had been able to produce.

But if the Monarch was victorious and happy, the Father was destined to experience a different fate. His ungrateful and unnatural son became his most implacable enemy. Several years had elapsed since his departure from court; the king had frequently commanded him to return, but in vain. His conquests over the English had even been impeded, and stopped in the mid-way, by a dangerous insurrection of the dauphin and duke of Savoy. Superadded to this, his exactions and oppressions in Dauphiné, where he exercised a sort of unlimited and royal power, were grown insupportable. Charles, irritated by such disobedience, and weary of his continued misconduct, commissioned the count de Dammartin to seize his person. That nobleman, whom he had formerly affronted in the tenderest part, proceeded instantly to the execution of the mandate; but

but Louis, who had received timely intelligence of the defign, faved himfelf by a precipitate flight into Franche Comté, from whence he continued his rout into Brabant.

The duke of Burgundy, either influenced by motives of generofity and courtefy, or from policy, received, and afforded him an afylum. He affigned him a penfion of twelve thoufand ecus, and gave him the Chateau de Gueneppe near Bruffels, for his refidence. Here he endeavoured at firft to amufe and divert his unquiet mind by the ftudy of aftrology, to which he was ever immoderately addicted; but afterwards, with that malevolent duplicity which fo ftrongly marked his character; and in defpite of all the benefits which the houfe of Burgundy had heaped upon him, he attempted to fow the feeds of difcontent and quarrel between the duke and his fon, the count de Charolois, in which he fucceeded but too well.

The king tried in vain by every means to induce the duke of Burgundy to deliver

ver up the dauphin. By a prediction founded on his knowledge of Louis, and juſtified in his future conduct, he warned him that he was nouriſhing a ſerpent, which when warmed would ſtrike his deadly fangs into the boſom of its protector. He even once was on the point of entering Flanders at the head of an army, to ſeize the rebellious prince; but renouncing his intentions, he determined rather to deprive him of the ſucceſſion, and to leave the crown to his younger ſon Charles duke of Berri. It is highly probable he would have effected this deſign, if death had not prevented him.

During the latter years of his life, Charles had become diſtruſtful, ſuſpicious, and uneaſy; he feared the dauphin's vindictive ſpirit might puſh him to attempts the moſt atrocious. While he reſided at Meun-ſur-Yeure, in Berri, he received repeated informations, that his own domeſtics had plotted to deſtroy him. The wretched king, terrified at an intimation ſo alarming, and not knowing on whoſe
 attachment

attachment or fidelity to repofe, refufed obftinately to receive any nourifhment during fome days; and when at length, vanquifhed by the importunity of his attendants, he would have willingly eat, nature was no longer able: he could not fwallow any fuftenance, and foon after expired.

The character of Charles is infinitely amiable. He poffeffed all thofe qualities which conciliate affection, and touch the heart. Courteous, gallant, liberal, amorous, and brave; yet finking, from natural difpofition, and a fort of yielding incapacity, into an effeminate and enervate indolence, which he could not refift; and again emerging into the exertion of all the virtues which diftinguifh a hero and a prince. Born to experience every viciffitude of fortune, and, after triumphing over his political enemies, to find domeftic ones more cruel and unfeeling, he may be accounted a happy monarch, but a miferable individual.

Though attached too clofely to his favourites,

vourites, and sometimes led by that attachment into errors, he yet never used his authority with rigour, or oppressed his people by heavy impositions: and his reign, distinguished by the entire extirpation of the English from the dominions of France, is one of those on which their historians peculiarly delight to dwell. The kingdom, long torn by every species of foreign and internal commotion, began to recover; and, no longer nourishing in its vitals a hostile and powerful enemy, grew more confirmed in its police, more important in the European scale. By a similar progression, the royal power, hitherto shackled and limited from the feudal regulations, acquiring gradually strength, became wider in its influence, and more resistless in its supremacy.—In the subsequent reign, it was carried into a despotism the most extensive and uncontrouled.

CHAPTER

CHAPTER THE THIRD.

Louis the eleventh's character, and commencement of his reign.—Interview with Henry king of Castile.—Louis's violence and oppressions.—League of the public good.—Accession and character of Charles, last duke of Burguudy.—Interview of Peronne.—King's imprisonment, and terrors.—Death of Charles duke of Berri.—Interview with Edward the fourth, at Pecquigni.—Louis's insidious policy.—The duke of Burgundy's attempts on Switzerland.—Battle of Nancy, and death.—Burgundy re-united to France.—Conclusion of Louis's reign.—Cruelties.—First stroke of an apoplexy.—His pilgrimage.—His encreasing severity.—Minute circumstances of his illness.—Death.—Character.—Mistresses.

WE are about to enter on a reign of a very extraordinary and singular nature. A prince odious in his character, detestable

KINGS OF FRANCE, &c. 77

deteftable in his conduct; violating every maxim of honourable or virtuous policy; deviating frequently even from the rules of intereft; uniformly flagitious, and fyftematically bad—yet attaining by the mazes of an infidious and eccentric fubtlety, to the completion of almoft all his views, and acquiring a prerogative and authority unknown to his predeceffors. Such is Louis the eleventh!—The detail of his actions as a king, will prove the juftice of the portrait.

So univerfally abhorred had the rebellion and ingratitude of Louis, while dauphin, rendered him, that a confiderable party was already formed in the court of Charles the feventh, for the young duke of Berri: but the count du Maine having fent intelligence to Louis of his father's death, he loft not a moment in profiting of it; and the duke of Burgundy, long his protector, and now become his vaffal, mounting on horfeback, attended him, together with his fon the count de Charolois, to Rheims,
where

where he caufed himfelf to be immediately crowned.

The opening of his reign was marked with all thofe changes and alterations cuftomary on the acceffion of princes; and peculiarly to be expected on that of one who had lived in open difcord with the preceding fovereign. Every maxim of government adopted by Charles, was counteracted by Louis; all his officers or favourites degraded with ignominy, and new ones advanced to power; the duke of Alençon, who had been committed to prifon for treafonable practices, releafed, and the count de Dammartin immured in the Baftile: the nobility difpoffeffed of their charges, and the people loaded with exactions: the duke of Bretagne invaded, and the duke of Berri defrauded of his appennage.

After a commencement fo ftrongly predictive of his future meafures, he haftened into Gafcony, to an interview with Henry the Impotent, king of Caftile. The two fovereigns met at Maüleon, on the
confines

confines of Navarre, and formed a contraſt not a little remarkable. Henry, vain, magnificent, haughty, and ſumptuous, attended with a ſplendid train. Louis, with no external marks of royalty; mean in his perſon; clad in coarſe cloth, ſhort and unbecoming: a notre dame of lead in his bonnet; and ſlenderly accompanied. After a fruitleſs conference, they both retired, with ſentiments of mutual contempt.

As he became confirmed in the throne, his character unfolded and developed itſelf. The labyrinths of a crooked policy in which he trod, made him ever attentive to the means of contracting and diminiſhing the power of all the great vaſſals of the crown. Among theſe, the duke of Burgundy held the firſt place; the duke of Bretagne the ſecond. With the former he exerted the arts of intrigue; and, by means of a ſecret correſpondence which he kept up in his court, procured the reſtitution of thoſe towns on the Somme, ceded at the treaty of Arras to Philip, and
which

which made him master of all Picardy. As this negociation was effected in contradiction to the sentiments of the count de Charolois, it laid the foundation of that personal hatred which he ever bore the king, and which Louis encreased by the tenor of all his subsequent conduct.

With the latter of these princes, as less powerful, he scarce observed any measures; the mandates he sent him, were of the most despotic and imperious nature; they forbad him to levy any taxes in his duchy, to strike money, or to term himself " duke, by the grace of God." It was, to deprive him at once of all independance, or sovereignty. Francis the second, a weak but generous prince, was at this time duke of Bretagne. Unable to refuse compliance with these haughty orders, he affected to submit to them; while he privately set on foot the means to restrain a power, which threatened the subversion or annihilation of every other.

Desirous to strengthen his proceedings by the shadow of a national concurrence, the

the king meanwhile aſſembled the ſtates, and laid before them his pretended reaſons for ſo unparalleled an act of deſpotiſm. Charles, duke of Orleans, firſt prince of the blood, reſpectable from his age, and beloved for his virtues, preſumed to oppoſe and diſapprove his meaſures; but the unfeeling Louis reproached and reprimanded him in expreſſions ſo cutting and ſevere, that the duke, unable to ſurvive this humiliating treatment, died of grief and mortification only two days after. His death did not obliterate his conduct, or ſoften the heart of his obdurate ſovereign: it was perpetuated in a breaſt which never forgave, and knew no emotions of tenderneſs, reſpected no ties of conſanguinity. The family of Orleans had pretenſions of the juſteſt kind on the duchy of Milan, in right of Valentina, mother of the deceaſed duke; but Louis, ſo far from eſpouſing theſe claims, allied himſelf with Franciſco Sforza, who had uſurped the dominions on the extinction of the houſe of Viſcomti, and ſecured him in poſſeſſion of them,

from

from motives of hatred to the princes of his own blood.

These reiterated and increasing acts of violence and oppression, produced in the end a general convulsion. The first nobles, roused by past indignities, and apprehensive of future ones more intolerable, took up arms against the author of them. The count de Dunois, grown grey under the late king, and universally revered, appeared at the head of his vassals: the count de St. Pol, and the duke of Nemours, were joined by Dammartin, escaped from his imprisonment. The duke of Bretagne prepared to enter France with an army; the duke of Berri fled to him for an asylum; and the count de Charolois, at the head of a considerable body of forces, directed his march strait to the capital.

In this alarming concurrence of circumstances, the genius of Louis, active, penetrating, and peculiarly calculated to extricate him from difficulties, eminently appeared. On the first news of the conspiracy, he fell immediately on the weakest leaders,

leaders, and reduced them to implore his clemency. The apprehenſion that his enemies might take poſſeſſion of Paris, obliged him to grant it; and he was on his way to ſecure that city, when the Burgundian army meeting him at Montlhery, an action unavoidably enſued. It was indeciſive; but the king, anxious for the preſervation of the metropolis, and diſtruſtful of the attachment of its citizens, firſt diſlodged, and re-entered Paris. Compelled by the neceſſity of his affairs, he bent with all the pliability of addreſs, adopted manners the moſt engaging and popular, courted the wives of the mechanics, promiſed a repeal of every onerous or extraordinary impoſt, and extended ſeveral acts of grace to retain them in allegiance.

Meanwhile the Breton army having joined the count de Charolois, formed a prodigious aſſemblage of troops: they aſſumed the title of the League for the public good; and directing their courſe towards the capital, encamped in the ſurrounding villages. After vainly attempting to gain poffeffion of it by blockade, or famine, or intrigue, and no infurrection taking place, terms of accommodation were propofed. Louis, who knew that this powerful combination could only be fuccefsfully reduced by effecting its difunion, complied with all their demands; refolved only to adhere to them, while compelled to it by force. He yielded therefore, though with infinite reluctance, the duchy of Normandy to Charles his brother; invefted the count de St. Pol with the fword of conftable; reftored the towns upon the Somme to the count de Charolois; and replaced the other chiefs of the confederacy in all their lands and offices. The league thus broken, each member of it returned into his own dominions or caftles; while the crafty king, only waiting for the favourable moment, held himfelf in readinefs, to improve it to the utmoft.

The infurrections of the Flemings againft the houfe of Burgundy, and the
difcontents

discontents of the Normans with the administration of their new duke, who suffered himself to be governed by weak counsellors, gave Louis that opportunity which he so anxiously desired. Vigorous and rapid in his movements when occasion demanded it, he first compelled the duke of Bretagne to abandon his brother; and then depriving the defenceless prince of his newly ceded duchy, forced him to fly a miserable refugee to his ally for shelter. The duke of Burgundy, broken with years and infirmities, could extend no protection to his friends in person; and his son was occupied with the rebellious Liègeois. They endeavoured to rouze the king of England in their quarrel; but Edward the fourth was as yet not sufficiently confirmed in the throne, to undertake a foreign war; and Louis, triumphant over so many enemies, and rendered stronger by their opposition, grew more tyrannical in his conduct, more oppressive in his government.

At this time Philip duke of Burgundy died

died in a very advanced age. His juftice, beneficence, and paternal attention to his people, obtained him the furname of "the Good." Superadded to thefe amiable qualifications, the extent of territory he poffeffed, and the fplendid munificence of his temper, ranked him among the greateft princes of his time. The count de Charolois his fon fucceeded him.—Of fiery and impetuous manners, bold even to temerity, inflexible in the profecution of defigns he had once adopted, aiming at royalty, and exhaufting his revenues in vain attempts to extend his dominions; Charles, over-reached in policy by the king of France, and unequal to the vaft projects he had conceived, deftroyed the fabric which his three predeceffors had erected, and expired the victim of his immoderate ambition.

Though Louis, from the prompt and immediate feizure of the occafion to attack the dukes of Bretagne and Berri, had gained the afcendency, yet this advantage was only temporary. Charles of Burgundy,

Burgundy, his inveterate enemy, was returned victorious from Flanders, and had reinspired the oppofition of his two allies, by leading a powerful army to their affiftance.

The king, wary and cautious, trufting no event to fortune which wifdom or fubtlety might regulate; and like Philip of Macedon, believing no fortrefs impregnable where a mule laden with filver could enter, attacked the duke firft with gold, and bought a truce at the price of one hundred and twenty thoufand ecus. As this however procured only a fufpenfion of hoftilities, and defirous of detaching him altogether from his connections, he determined on a perfonal interview: relying on his own powers of perfuafion, and duped by his vanity, Louis named Peronne as the place of their meeting. Willing at the fame time to give the duke an inconteftible proof of his perfect confidence in his honour, he came without any guards, and only attended by two or three noblemen of his court. Charles received

ceived him with every mark of honorary diftinction, and lodged him in the town; but feveral Burgundian and other foreign perfons of rank arriving, who were his avowed enemies, he began to entertain fome apprehenfions refpecting his fafety, and requefted the duke to affign him apartments in the caftle, as more fecure from infult or injury. By this ftep, ftill more imprudent than the firft, he rendered himfelf abfolutely a prifoner.

Previous to the interview, the king, whofe grand object was ever to keep the duke of Burgundy employed in domeftic wars, had fent agents privately to Liège, to induce them to refume their arms, by a promife of his protection. He did not expect the confequence of this meffage to be inftantaneous; but the Liègeois impetuous and violent, no fooner received the intimation, than they broke out into open rebellion, maffacred their governors, and committed a thoufand exceffes. When Charles received this intelligence, he became furious with refentment. Perfectly
confcious

conscious at whose instigation it had been commenced, he denounced vengeance against the perfidious monarch, ordered the castle gates to be closed, and even debated whether he should not put him to immediate death.

Louis, naturally timid and irresolute, in the hands of his mortal enemy whom he had deeply offended, surrounded with people who detested him, and shut up in a chamber at the foot of that very tower where Hebert, count de Vermandois, had formerly caused Charles the Simple to be murdered, underwent by anticipation all the horrors of death. The duke kept him three days in this painful suspence; during which time, the king, whose subtlety forsook him not in so dangerous a crisis, found means to engage some of his attendants in his interests. He was released; but under conditions the most ignominious and humiliating. Charles obliged the king to accompany him with three hundred men at arms to the siege of Liège, which he took by storm, punished
with

with extreme severity their disobedience; and then dismissing his sovereign, whom he had compelled to be a witness of all these transactions, he scarce deigned to accompany him half a league on his way, and bid him adieu with a sort of haughty civility.

There is no incident of Louis's reign, no action in his conduct, so apparently contradictory to his character, as his behaviour in this celebrated interview: his sagacity and his cautious temper bordering on fear, seem equally to have forsaken him; and the prince of his age the most crafty and political, suffered himself to be over-reached by one the least endowed with those qualities.

Among the articles to which the king was reduced to submit while at Peronne, he had promised to cede Champagne and Brie to his brother; but as the vicinity of these provinces to the Burgundian dominions rendered it highly hazardous, and would have infallibly secured the alliance between the two dukes; Louis no sooner

sooner effected his escape, than he exerted every engine of dexterity to prevail on his brother to accept Guyenne in exchange. The young prince, weak, and yielding to the affected demonstrations of kindness shewn him, complied with the proposal; but convinced when too late of the error he had committed, and allured by the hopes of a marriage with Mary of Burgundy, Charles's only daughter, and heiress of his vast possessions, he began to renew his confederacy with him, and to raise troops,—His death, marked with every appearance of poison, and the evident interest which Louis had to perpetrate this crime, superadded to the personal hatred he bore the duke, conspired to render him justly and universally suspected of the fact *. Guyenne was immediately

---

* The duke of Berri appears to have been an amiable prince, but of slender capacity. Alternately the slave of devotion and of love, he was governed by his confessor or his mistress, according to his predominant weakness. The latter prevailed;
and

mediately feized, and re-united to the crown.

The news of this deplorable and unexpected event no fooner reached the duke of Burgundy, than all his indignation and refentment revived. He entered Pi-

and the lady of Montforeau triumphed over the abbot of St. John d'Angeli. Jealous of this pre-eminence, and bent on revenge, the monk caufed a peach to be poifoned, which he prefented to the lady. She divided it with a knife, and giving half to her lover, eat the reft herfelf: the confequence was immediately fatal, and fhe expired in great agonies. The duke, from the ftrength of his conftitution, refifted the poifon, during fome time; though he loft his hair and nails which came off, yet he lingered near fix months, and then died at Bourdeaux. The abbot fled; but being feized in Bretagne by order of Francis the fecond, the reigning duke, he was carried to Nantes; it was intended to bring him to a public trial, in the hope and expectation of his accufing Louis the eleventh, as his accomplice or abettor — but on the morning appointed to conduct him before the judges, he was found dead in his cell, ftrangled and lying on the floor. As by this cataftrophe, a veil was drawn before the whole affair, it was commonly believed that the king had not hefitated to conceal the firft crime by the perpetration of a fecond.

cardy

cardy with an army, determined to revenge his unhappy ally, to whofe manes he facrificed every inhabitant who fell into his power; but having failed in an attempt on Beauvais, and exhaufting his forces by efforts of a vain and impotent frenzy, rather than of a manly vengeance, he was foon under a neceffity of accepting the truce which Louis offered him. This latter prince, uniform and fyftematical in his movements; ever attaining his ends by thofe means which feemed moft remote from their object, grew every year more defpotic, and added fome new acquifition to the regal prerogative or authority: he feized on the territories of the count d'Armagnac, committed the duke of Alençon to prifon, and retained the duke of Bretagne in his fubjection.

While Louis thus aggrandized his houfe, the duke of Burgundy, whom a fatal paffion for extending his dominions had intoxicated, began that train of errors and mifconduct which terminated in his fall. Inftead of watching with circumfpection spection the minutest actions of his perfidious and powerful neighbour; he engaged in a quarrel with the whole Germanic body, by laying siege to Nuiz on the Rhine, under pretexts the most insufficient, and even persisted in it to the destruction of his whole army, without success.

In the mean time, Edward the fourth, having vanquished all the partizans of the house of Lancaster, and established himself in the throne, began to turn his view to the recovery of those possessions, to which every king of England since Edward the third had laid claim. Endowed with martial qualities, successful in every war where he had personally commanded, and yet in the vigour of his age, he seemed capable of renewing the laurels won at Azincourt. Invited by the pressing and repeated importunities of the duke of Burgundy, he landed at Calais; but his ally, engaged in the siege of Nuiz, and pertinaciously adhering to his design, after detaining him some time, appeared unattended

tended and single, instead of bringing, according to promise, a powerful body of troops. Edward however advanced into Picardy, in the expectation that the constable St. Pol would, as he had promised, surrender into their hands the town of St. Quintin; but the count, by a double piece of treachery, deceived his allies, and gave Louis time to avert the storm.

The subtle king had recourse to artifice and negotiation, his usual engines; he knew that the decision of arms was ever hazardous and uncertain; that of intrigue, more sure and unfailing. Edward, voluptuous and indolent, lent an easy ear to these proposals; an accommodation was soon managed, and a peace signed, notwithstanding Charles's opposition, at Amiens. The two monarchs in consequence agreed on an interview at the bridge of Pecquigni, near that city. A grated barrier was erected on the middle, and two boxes raised for the purpose. Louis, whose pliant genius accommodated itself to every situation of politics, and

who

who thought no fubmiffions too mean for the attainment of his views; flattered the Englifh prince, invited him with all the apparent cordiality of friendfhip to his capital, and at the fame time fecured by prefents the principal nobles in his interefts.

Edward returned to England; the Burgundian, compelled by neceffity and weaknefs, accepted a fufpenfion of arms; and the conftable, whofe perfidy had rendered him obnoxious to every party, was given up by Charles into the king's hands, who after a hafty trial, caufed him to be condemned for treafon, and inftantly beheaded.

Untaught by the ill fuccefs which had attended all his plans of ambition and greatnefs, the duke of Burgundy perfifted in the purfuit of them. He engaged in a difpute with the Swifs cantons, nor would hearken to the humble and repeated inftances they made to him for peace. Thefe virtuous and hardy people, who had purchafed their freedom by the boldeft

oppofition

opposition to Austrian tyranny, and who cherished amid their lakes and mountains the warmest attachment to it, resisted his invasion with determined courage; and after having defeated him in two engagements, obliged him to renounce his enterprize with ignominy.

Still bent on conquests, and driven almost to madness by his repeated disgraces, he laid siege to Nancy in Lorrain, though with only three thousand men, and amid the rigours of winter. René duke of Lorrain attacked him with superior forces. At the first shock, the count de Campobasso, a Neapolitan, on whom he had conferred unnumbered favours, basely withdrew with four hundred horse which he commanded; and at the same time, by an act of unparalleled ingratitude and villainy, left twelve or fifteen men about his person, with strict command to assassinate him in his flight. They executed the detestable commission but too faithfully; and the unhappy duke was found dead, pierced with three wounds. — It is not certain

MEMOIRS OF THE

certain what motive influenced Campobaſſo to perpetrate ſo foul a crime on his benefactor. It is ſaid, that Charles had once ſtruck him, and that revenge ſtimulated him to it; but hiſtory has not clearly elucidated this point*.

Thus

---

* Campobaſſo had been baniſhed from Naples, on account of his adherence to the Angevine faction in that kingdom. From whatever ſource his hatred to the duke of Burgundy originated, he carried it to the moſt flagitious pitch, ſince he certainly offered Louis the eleventh, repeatedly, to deliver up to him his maſter alive or dead. The king, how little ſcrupulous ſoever to circumvent his enemies, abhorred ſo black a treachery, and even ſent Charles intimation of the deſign—but the infamous opinion which he entertained of the perſon from whom this information came, made him neglect and deſpiſe it. "If," ſaid he, "it were true, the king would never have "imparted to me ſo important a ſecret." He even redoubled his marks of confidence and attachment to the perfidious Neapolitan.

His body, though carefully ſought for, could not be diſcovered, after the action, till Campobaſſo ſent an Italian page, who pointed out the ſpot where he fell, which was at ſome diſtance from the ſcene of battle. The duke was entirely naked, lying on his

belly,

KINGS OF FRANCE, &c. 99

Thus fell the laſt male of the great houſe of Burgundy. Mary, his only daughter,

belly, and his face cloſe to a piece of ice of the marſh where he had expired. He was wounded in three places: one, by a halberd, which had ſplit his jaw; the two others were made by a pike; the firſt having pierced both his thighs from ſide to ſide, and the laſt entered a little higher. The duke of Lorrain cauſed him to be tranſported to Nancy, and laid on a bed of ſtate, in an apartment hung with black velvet. He afterwards paid him the cuſtomary funeral honours, which were of a moſt ſingular nature.—René wore on that occaſion a golden beard reaching to his middle. Previous to his ſcattering holy water on the corpſe, he advanced up to the deceaſed prince, and taking him by the hand, addreſſed him in theſe words— "God reſt thy ſoul; thou haſt given us much "trouble and grief!"

Charles's errors and vices ſeem to have been more pernicious to himſelf, than injurious to others. He poſſeſſed many ſublime and ſhining qualities; among which his undaunted intrepidity, liberality, application, and magnificence were peculiarly eminent. He was of a middle ſtature, and vigorous frame of body, capable of great fatigue. The lineaments of his countenance were harſh and unpleaſing; his phyſiognomy appearing to indicate the fierceneſs of his natural diſpoſition.——Theſe circumſtances of the

H 2   duke's

daughter, who had not yet attained her twentieth year, was unable to affert her title to the ample poffeffions which devolved to her. The imprudence and misfortunes of her father had left the ftate exhaufted and impotent; the treafury empty; a council difmayed and feeble; troops almoft exterminated.—In this dif-

duke's character and death are chiefly borrowed from Cominés.

The " Chronique fcandaleufe," written by John de Troyes, agrees with the laft-mentioned hiftorian in almoft every particular, and adds fome others not lefs curious.—" Charles's body," fays he, " was
" diftinguifhed from the others that lay near it in
" the fame ftate of nakednefs, by fix marks, which
" infallibly afcertained his identity. The firft was,
" the want of his upper teeth, which had been
" beaten out by a fall; the fecond was, a fcar on
" his throat, occafioned by a wound he received at
" the battle of Montlhery; the third, his great
" nails, which he always wore longer than any of
" his courtiers; fourthly, another fcar on his left
" fhoulder; the fifth was, a fiftula on his right
" groin; and laftly, a nail of his foot that grew
" into his little toe.—His phyfician, chaplain, and
" gentlemen of his bed-chamber recognized their
" mafter by thefe marks."

treffed

treffed fituation, fhe implored the protection of Louis; fhe fubmitted herfelf and her dominions to his pleafure; fhe even preffingly requefted, that by a marriage with a prince of France, her territories might be re-united to the crown in all their branches.—The conduct of the king to the young princefs, on this occafion, was equally deftitute of magnanimity, as of true policy. To the former fentiment he was ever a ftranger; but nothing, except his unrelenting deteftation of the Burgundian race, and that eccentric, peculiar path in which he delighted to tread, could have induced him to prefer the hoftile feizure of a part of her dominions, to the tranquil and undifputed poffeffion of the whole. Such was however the alternative he chofe! His army immediately rendered themfelves mafters of Burgundy almoft without oppofition.

The unprotected duchefs, whofe condition, fo juftly excitive of compaffion, could not foften the malignant heart of Louis, was neceffitated, after a number of delays and

and irresolutions, to accept the hand of Maximilian, son to the emperor Frederic; who was by no means capable of recovering her dismembered territories from so powerful an antagonist. The king of England was bound by every principle of generosity and wisdom, to assist and support her declining fortunes; but Louis, subtle and provident, had precluded this channel of succour, by a promise of the dauphin to Edward's eldest daughter, tho' without any intention of fulfilling it: and after some feeble and ineffectual efforts on the part of Maximilian, all Burgundy and Artois remained to France.

As Louis advanced in years, the vices of his nature growing inveterate, obtained the fullest command over him. The despotism which he had established, leaving no barrier to his authority, unveiled and gave full scope to that implacable cruelty which characterised him through every stage of life. He had preserved an unceasing desire of vengeance against the duke of Nemours ever since the war of the Public Good;

Good; and was now determined to gratify it. That unfortunate nobleman, dreading his sovereign's resentment, had retired to the fortress of Carlat, among the mountains of Auvergne. Louis sent the Seigneur de Beaujeu, to whom he had married his daughter Anne, with orders to invest him in it; but the inacceffible situation of the castle rendering it very difficult to gain possession by force, the duke received the most solemn assurances of safety, if he would surrender. Reposing on the honour of his enemy, he complied: but the king, who sported with all the ties of virtue and society, caused him, in violation of his compact, to be carried to the Bastile; he then compelled, though with difficulty, the reluctant judges to condemn him, and ordered him to be beheaded. Nor did his revenge stop there; but, by a refinement in cruelty unexampled, he commanded the two sons of the duke, yet in early childhood, and of consequence incapable of any participation in treason, to be placed directly under the scaffold, and covered with the

the blood of their miserable father, which descended on their heads.

These are recitals at which humanity shudders; but what shall we say to the universal testimony of the French historians, and even of Cominés himself; who assure, that during his reign, he put to death more than four thousand persons by various species of torture, without even the forms of trial; and that he usually was present himself at their executions, in which spectacle he tasted a barbarous satisfaction? Scarce do the frantic excesses of Caligula surpass those of Louis in atrocity or number. Happily we draw towards the termination of this tragic drama.

While every public and private prosperity seemed to attend on the king, and no foreign or internal commotion disturbed his schemes, death prepared to arrest him. He was at a village near Chinon in Touraine, when a stroke of an apoplexy seized him: he lay two days motionless and speechless; at the end of which time, his voice and intellects returned, but not the

health

health he had previoufly enjoyed. Rendered more diftruftful by this fymptom of approaching diffolution, and jealous left from any perfonal incapacity, attempts fhould be made to infringe his authority; he redoubled his vigilance and timid circumfpection. As the duke of Bourbon appeared to be the only prince who poffeffed the qualities requifite for fuch a pretenfion, he feized, without accufal or pretext, on all his lands; and even endeavoured to invent crimes by which he might ultimately ruin and put him to death.

Amid thefe occupations, a fecond apopleétic feizure again warned him of his end. To avert the impending calamity, he made a pilgrimage to St. Claude in Franche Comté : his devotion and his cruelty both increafed; he was attended in this mock pilgrimage by fix thoufand men at arms, and left bloody traces of his rout in almoft every place through which he paffed.

So far from relaxing his accuftomed feverity, as he approached the verge of life, his

his temper hardened into a sterner barbarity. His wife, whose patient and enduring attachment, whose mild and silent virtues, merited a better treatment, he banished into Savoy, after having kept her during many years shut up in some one of the royal castles; where he rarely visited her, and in which she resided as a simple individual, without state, and almost without attendants. By his last will, he expresly precluded her from any share in the government, and endeavoured to inspire his son with sentiments of distrust and aversion to his mother.

The young dauphin he held as a sort of prisoner in the castle of Amboise, where he saw none except valets and persons of the meanest condition. No education, no instructions were infused into his early mind, from a dread, that such information might awaken his dormant qualities, and induce him to make attempts against the government.

His treatment of Louis duke of Orleans, first prince of the blood, was similar.

lar. He carried him with him a captive wherever he moved; and, by one of those abominable strokes of unnatural policy which discriminate Louis the eleventh from any other monarch, he obliged him to marry the princess Jane, his youngest daughter; though she was deformed in a great degree, and had not even received a decent education. She was besides only twelve years of age, and the duke only fourteen. This union of force and compulsion was afterwards broken by Louis, when he ascended the throne *.

Besides

---

* There are some circumstances so curious and extraordinary, relative to this marriage, that I cannot dispense with mentioning them. It seems that the king was fully convinced his daughter could bear no children, since, in a letter of his to the count de Dammartin still extant, he says, speaking of the future bride and her husband,—" Qu'ils n'auroient pas " beaucoup d'embarras à nourrir les enfans qui naî- " troient de leur union; mais cependant, elle aura " lieu, quelque chose qu'on en puisse dire."

Louis the twelfth pretended that he never consummated the nuptials; but this, on many accounts, is highly improbable, though admitted by pope Alexander

der

Befides thefe inftances of domeftic tyranny, the people groaned under his oppreffions. Numbers of the nobility were carried about as wild beafts, confined in iron cages; a horrid invention, unknown before this reign, and the frequency of which increafed with the progrefs of his diforder. A third ftroke, of a fimilar nature with the two former, feemed to promife his kingdom a termination of its evils; yet he ftill furvived for new feverities.

The death of Charles of Anjou at this juncture added Provence to the crown; and that of Mary of Burgundy, who pe-

---

der the fixth, at the fubfequent diffolution of them. St. Gelais de Montlieu, in his hiftory, exprefsly afferts the contrary: thefe are his words — " C'eft grand
" merveille de ce qu'on faifoit au duc d'Orleans, et
" les menaces qu'on lui faifoit s'il ne s'acquittoit de
" coucher avec la dite dame Jehanne. On ne le
" menaçoit de rien moins que de la vie; et j'aurois
" grand honte de reciter la façon comme on ufoient
" ceux qui étoient autour, tant hommes que femmes."
—All this plainly befpeaks the confummation of their marriage.

rifhed

rished by a fall from her horse in hunting, during her pregnancy*, opened the way to a pacification between Louis and Maximilian, by the affiance of his infant daughter Margaret with the dauphin Charles.

Edward the fourth expired much about the same time; and England by that event, was once more plunged into all those convulsions and civil broils, from which she had hardly begun to recover.

The concluding scenes of Louis's life hold up one of the most awful pictures

---

* Cominés says, she died of a fever consequent to, and occasioned by her accident. The cotemporary authors assert, that her exquisite modesty and delicacy alone made the fall fatal; since she preferred death to the permitting a surgeon to set her thigh, which was broke.

Her subjects deeply regretted her loss.—She had rendered herself universally beloved for her affability, liberality, and faithful attachment to her husband.— Lord Rivers, brother to Elizabeth Woodville, Edward the fourth's queen, had been among the number of her suitors; but was refused, as of a rank too much beneath the princess.

which

which can be prefented to the imagination. That of Pygmalion, though heightened by the colours of Fenelon's rich and defcriptive pen, is not more tremendous, or more affecting. He exhaufted every power of medicine, or devotion, or artifice, to prolong a miferable and hateful exiftence. To infpire him with gaiety, the moft beautiful country girls were brought to dance round his houfe, and bands of men who played on lutes accompanied them. To intercede with Heaven in his behalf, proceffions were ordered throughout the whole kingdom for his recovery; and public prayers offered, to avert the Bize, a cold, piercing wind which incommoded him extremely. A vaft collection of relics was brought, as if to fecure him by their influence from the ftroke of death: while his phyfician treated him with infult, and extorted from him vaft fums of money; which the king dared not to refufe him in thofe circumftances. It is even pretended, that a bath of infant's blood was prepared for him, in the expectation

pectation that it would foften the acrimony of his fcorbutic humours; but to this we may lend a very flender faith.

After changing his place of refidence many times, he fat down at the caftle of Plefliz-les-Tours. The walls were covered with iron fpikes; a guard of crofs-bow men watched night and day, as if to fecure him from invafion. He heard enemies in the paffing wind: every thing terrified and alarmed his guilty mind. Only one wicket admitted into the caftle; and fcarce any one approached his perfon, except the lady of Beaujeu his daughter, and her hufband. During thefe difmal circumftances, he yet tried to perfuade himfelf and others that he might live. In this flattering delufion, he fent to feek a Calabrian hermit, eminent for fanctity, named Francifco de Paolo. He threw himfelf on his knees before this monk; befought with humble fupplications his intereft with the Deity for the prolongation of his life; built him two convents, as proofs of his zeal; and knew no bounds to his adulation

lation and refpect for the fuppofed minifter of Heaven.

Finding however the inevitable hour of fate advance, and unable longer to turn his eyes from the furvey of it; he fent for Charles, his fon, from Amboife, and gave him fome falutary advice, exactly oppofite to the uniform tenor of all his own conduct — to cherifh the princes of the blood; to govern by the advice of his nobles; not to controvert the eftablifhed laws; and to diminifh the exorbitant impofts with which he had burdened his fubjects. This was the concluding act of his life: he expired fome days after.

Thofe who are converfant in the great works of antiquity, will be ftrikingly reminded, on the perufal of this ftory, of the defcription of Tiberius's exit, as related by Tacitus. It feems marked with all the fame ftrokes of character.——
" Jam Tiberium corpus, jam vires, non-
" dum diffimulatio deferebat. Idem a-
" nimi rigor, fermone ac vultu intentus,
" quæfita interdum comitate, quamvis
" manifeftam

"manifestam defectionem tegebat; mutatisque sæpius locis, tandem apud promontorium Miseni confedit."

After so minute and diffuse a narration of Louis the eleventh's conduct and death, it will be needless to draw the character of the king with equal accuracy. The principal strokes of it cannot be mistaken. His virtues, if he can be said to have possessed any, were those of policy and artifice: his vices, of disposition and the heart. Even his understanding, though clear, sagacious, and discerning, was frequently so fine and subtle, that it misled him by its own cunning, and overshot his purposes. France however continued to rise in the scale of empire. Charles the seventh laid the foundation of this aggrandisement, by his expulsion of the English. Louis added Burgundy, Artois, and Provence to the crown. Only Bretagne remained, of the great fiefs, unannexed.

The malignant and unamiable character of Louis did not prevent him from some gallant-

gallantries. History has preserved the names of several successive mistresses to whom he was attached. Margaret de Saffenage is the most known and celebrated: she died before his accession to the crown; but we never find that any of them influenced the king, or assumed the least command over affairs of state. By his first wife, the princess Margaret of Scotland, he had no issue; nor does it appear that he even consummated the marriage, or cohabited with her, on account of some secret defect in her person *. His queen, Charlotte of Savoy, an amiable woman, only survived him three months.

I have

* She was daughter to James the first, and only eleven years old when married to Louis, then dauphin, at Tours. What the peculiar object of her husband's disgust and aversion was, seems covered up very mysteriously, and is hard to ascertain. Most of the cotemporary authors assert, that her breath was very disagreeable, and that from that cause arose his estrangement to her. Cominés only says, Louis never loved her; without assigning the reason.—She was an accomplished princess in other respects, and protected letters.

I have permitted myſelf to run into a greater prolixity on this reign, than I generally intend—poſſibly greater than was requiſite. I mean to intereſt, rather than inſtruct; and this end can only be attained by an enumeration of thoſe ſeemingly trifling circumſtances; which yet often diſplay the picture of human nature with more fidelity, than the greater actions of the monarch, obſcured by the veil of policy.

letters. A ſingular anecdote is related of her, ſtrongly corroborating this.

Paſſing accidentally through an apartment where Alain Chartier, the moſt brilliant genius but the uglieſt man of his age, lay aſleep, ſhe advanced up to him and kiſſed him—Her ladies reproaching her by their looks for this ſeeming violation of female modeſty; "It was not the man," ſaid ſhe, "whom I kiſſed, "but the mouth from whence have proceeded ſo "many elevated ſentiments."

She died at Chalons-ſur-Mane, about five years after her marriage, without iſſue; and, as the French authors inform us, of grief for the calumnious imputations affixed on her honour,

CHAPTER THE FOURTH.

Acceſſion of Charles the eighth.—Character of the regent, Anne, lady of Beaujeu.— Her adminiſtration. — Attempts on the duchy of Bretagne.—The duke of Orleans's intrigues and flight.—His impriſonment. —Marriage of Anne of Bretagne to the king.—The duchy united to the crown.— Termination of the regency.—Charles's opening character.—He is inflamed with ſchemes of conqueſt. — Attack on the kingdom of Naples.—Romantic expedition. —His march — Uninterrupted train of victory—Coronation—Return.—Battle of Fornoua.—Charles abandons himſelf to pleaſures.—Naples loſt.—New plans of invaſion.—Renounced.—The king's change, and ſudden death.—Circumſtances of it.— Character.

THE age of Charles the eighth, at his acceſſion to the crown, was of that critical nature, which rendered it difficult to provide for the regulation of the ſtate.

He

He might be reputed a major without any confiderable violence to the forms of the monarchy, fince he had nearly completed his fourteenth year;—but the meannefs of his education, the confinement to which he had always been fubjected, and his feeble conftitution, delicate and fickly, feemed to demand fome abler and more experienced conductor. The late king, whofe views ever piercing and active forefaw this neceffity, had not failed to apply to it a remedy. In his expiring moments he nominated Anne, his eldeft daughter, to the firft charge of the government, though with the title, not of regent, but of governefs.

The princefs had received from nature all the qualities requifite for this high office. A genius equal to her father's: more uniformity of conduct, and greater magnanimity of mind. Her judgment was found, without any mixture of that perfidious duplicity which debafed the underftanding of Louis. Though vindictive, not cruel; though tenacious of her dignity,

dignity, not violent or imperious. Led by no inferior paffions, fhe felt her capacities for adminiftration, and facrificed fovereignly to this purfuit. Miftrefs of eloquence, and addrefs the moft refined, fhe knew how to poffefs, and to retain the authority delegated to her.—Such are the bold and vivid colours under which the cotemporary writers have tranfmitted to us her character; and we find them fully expanded and difplayed during the fhort but vigorous period, when fhe poffeffed the fupreme command of affairs.

But though talents fo various and exalted appeared to juftify the confidence repofed in her by Louis the eleventh, equity and uniform prefcription feemed to call Louis duke of Orleans to the helm of ftate. His rank, as firft prince of the blood, and even prefumptive heir to the crown, rendered his claim incontrovertible; if his unripe age, which exceeded not twenty years, did not diminifh the force of this plea. Anne knew how to avail herfelf of the defect; and, by an exertion

of

of that dexterity and management which she so eminently poffeffed, fecured to herself, notwithftanding the duke's oppofition, the poft with which she had been invefted.

Her firft acts were of the moft ingratiating and popular nature. Several creatures, rather than minifters, of the late king, who had abufed their favour, by the commiffion of crimes the moft enormous, she furrendered up to public punifhment. She revoked the donations which his fuperftition and terrors of approaching death had induced him to make to feveral convents and monaftic orders; and conciliated univerfal favour by a mild and equal government. Thefe were however only the inferior operations of the cabinet. Anne, more daring and intrepid than her father, faw that the favourable moment was at hand, to reunite Bretagne to the crown of France; nor was deterred from the profecution of her plan, by the obftacles which environed it.

Francis the fecond, funk into years and imbecility, had refigned all power into the hands of Landais; whom an infinuating and flexible genius, calculated to rife in courts, had promoted from a mechanical occupation, to the difpofal of all his mafter's favour. The Breton nobility, incenfed at fo unworthy a choice, and irritated by the acts of oppreffion and violence which he committed, endeavoured to effect his fall; but the duke, attached to his favourite, fheltered him from their indignation. Landais, not content with an efcape, was defirous of revenge: he menaced his enemies, and even proceeded to the execution of his threats. Neceffity, united to the defire of vengeance, forced them to recur for protection to the French miniftry; and Anne, who only waited for the application, was ready to grant their requefts of affiftance; when fome oppofition which fhe met with from another quarter, compelled her to turn her views that way, and relinquifh for an inftant her project.

Though

KINGS OF FRANCE, &c. 121

Though the superior address and policy of his rival, had obliged the duke of Orleans to acquiesce in her nomination to the first post of state; yet his disappointed ambition, in so important a struggle, had tended to nourish in his bosom an animosity to her; and his temper, open, and incapable of disguise, made him careless or inattentive to its concealment. An incident small in itself, but attended with very important consequences, displayed his resentment, and hastened the reduction of Bretagne.

The court was at Melun. The duke of Orleans and some other young noblemen were engaged in a party at tennis, of which the king and his sister were spectators: a dispute arising relative to a stroke which involved the decision of the game, it was referred to them. Madame de Beaujeu hesitated not to pronounce in the duke's disfavour; who, incensed at what he apprehended to be an act of flagrant injustice, and the result of personal enmity, was so imprudent as to say, in a tone of voice by no

no means inaudible, "Que quiconque
" l'avoit condamné, fi c'étoit un homme,
" il en avoit menti; et fi c'étoit une
" femme, que c'étoit une putaine."—This
affront, which was of the groffeft nature,
became unpardonable, when offered to fo
great a perfonage, and in the royal prefence. Anne, miftrefs of her indignation,
reftrained it fo far as not to order his immediate arreft: but fhe procured from the
council an order for that purpofe, which
would have been carried into prompt execution, if the duke had not fecured himfelf by flight, and affembled his partizans
and vaffals for his defence. It was vain.
She befieged him in Beaugency on the
Loire; reduced him to terms of abfolute
fubmiffion; and left him no other authority than that which his rank alone procured.

Louis, though impatient of a yoke fo
galling, was not in a condition to fhake it
off; he even affected an entire acquief-
cence: but Anne, jealous and vigilant, having received information that he had entered

tered into some negociations with the duke of Bretagne, sent him an order to repair instantly to the king; and, on his attempting by a messenger to excuse himself under frivolous pretexts, commanded the marechal de Gié to conduct him to her. The duke obeyed, and began his journey: but having gone out next morning, under pretence of trying some new falcons, he escaped a second time, and gained the territories of his ally Francis; who promised him his daughter Anne, heiress to the duchy, in marriage, and entered into the closest connections with him.

The nobility of Bretagne, who had incensed their prince by the destruction and death of his favourite Landais; apprehensive of a severe chastisement by this accession of strength, implored protection from the lady of Beaujeu. She marched instantly a considerable army to their rescue; and, after several inferior advantages, gained the celebrated battle of St. Aubin du Cormier, which decided the contest. The duke of Orleans, who fought on foot, and

and behaved with diſtinguiſhed courage, was taken priſoner. After a ſhort confinement at the caſtle of Luſignan in Poictou, he was conducted to Bourges, where he remained a captive in the great tower above two years.

The ſucceſſes of the French arms obliged Madame de Beaujeu to unmaſk, and declare openly to the Breton nobility, who preſſed her to withdraw her troops, that it was now no longer time. An avowal ſo declaratory of the intention to annex the duchy for ever to the crown, re-united every diſaffected perſon, and reſtored to the duke his rebellious nobility. But Francis, overcome with infirmities, and hurt by a fall from his horſe, expired at this juncture; and left his daughter Anne, ſcarce thirteen years of age, ſurrounded with dangers and enemies.

New factions, and new competitors aroſe for this rich alliance.—The Seigneur d'Albret had ſeveral partizans. Maximilian, who had been married to Mary of Burgundy, aſpired to her hand: nor was the

KINGS OF FRANCE, &c.

the duke of Orleans's party, if he had not been detained a prisoner, yet extinct. The young princess decided in favour of the archduke; and the marriage was not only solemnized by proxy, but attended with a singular and curious ceremony; that of the count de Nassau's introducing his naked leg into the bed of the bride, as representing the person of Maximilian. Had he come himself in person, as every principle of policy dictated, the union would have been rendered indissoluble; but the abject, and almost incredible parsimony of the emperor Frederic, his father, who refused him the inconsiderable sum of two thousand ecus, on this great occasion, deprived him of an acquisition so important.

The French council, fearful lest the prize should be lost amid so many intrigues and delays, determined to send back the princess Margaret of Austria, to whom the king had been long betrothed, and to demand Anne of Bretagne for Charles the eighth; but though pressed

preſſed by the moſt urgent neceſſity, and inveſted by the forces of the ſovereign who courted her alliance, ſhe diſdained to violate the faith ſhe had once pledged; and refuſed, with a noble perſeverance, to accept any huſband except the one ſhe had already choſen. Attacked however on every ſide, and even entreated by the duke of Orleans, whom Charles took from priſon, and ſent to urge his ſuit; and on the other hand, diſguſted by the coldneſs and tardineſs of the archduke, who did not manifeſt the anxiety or impatience which ſuch a match might juſtly excite; the young ducheſs yielded at length, and the nuptials were celebrated at Langeais in Touraine. Maximilian exclaimed loudly againſt this double infringement of the moſt ſolemn and binding inſtitutions; but the evil was irremediable, and the laſt great fief ſwallowed up in the dominions of France.

Henry the ſeventh of England, who had acted, from motives of avarice, a part ſimilar to that which Edward the fourth

fourth had taken in the affairs of Mary of Burgundy, rather affected to make, than really made, an effort for the preservation of the duchy. He landed at Calais; but was soon induced to retire into his own dominions, by an argument irresistible with a prince of his character—I mean gold.

With the important acquisition of Bretagne, may be said to have terminated the authority of Anne de Beaujeu. Her credit and influence had begun previously to diminish. The young king, who approached to years of manhood, manifested too great an impatience of controul, to be longer held in tutelage; and his character expanding with his age, rendered him known to his people. No resemblance of his father appeared in Charles. Lively and brilliant, but of feeble judgment, he possessed a temper the most amiable and gentle; a heart which even power could not corrupt to the commission of a crime. Fond of pleasure, though easily inflamed with the love of glory,

glory, he facrificed alternately to both; and refembled his grandfather, Charles the feventh, in the rapid tranfitions he made from one to the other.

During the interval of tranquillity and repofe which fucceeded to the reduction or union of Bretagne; the courtiers, defirous of ingratiating themfelves with their fovereign, began firft to dazzle his imagination with ideas of fame and conqueft. The pretenfions which, as fucceffor to the houfe of Anjou, he had on the kingdom of Naples, formed a plaufible and flattering theme to a youthful mind. Charles poffeffed the perfonal courage requifite for military exploits. Ludovico Sforza, furnamed the Moor, brother to the celebrated Francifco, and uncle to the reigning duke of Milan, Galeazzo, invited and importuned him, from interefted motives, to come and take poffeffion of his right. Upon the firft report of fuch an intention, Ferdinand, who reigned in Naples, and who had paffed his feventieth year, fent an embaffy to the king, of the moft fubmif-
five

five nature, offering to pay homage, and an annual tribute. These proposals, which ought to have been accepted, were instantly refused; and the old king, terrified at the impending invasion, and unable to avert it, expired soon after of grief and terror.

The rage for foreign war having once gained possession of the young monarch, no arguments or motives of policy could induce him to relinquish it. In vain did the lady of Beaujeu oppose so rash and ill-concerted an enterprize. She had lost her former influence, and was no longer heard. With such warmth was this injudicious determination adopted, that even the most important and certain acquisitions were renounced, for a contingent and distant crown. Roussillon and Cerdagne, of which Louis the eleventh had possessed himself during the troubles of Spain, by an unwearied and masterly policy, were ceded to Ferdinand of Arragon, only to obtain his neutrality in the attack on Naples. None of the absurd and legendary adventures of chivalry were ever more romantic, or undertaken in greater contradiction to reason, than this of Charles. Without money, without any certain or honourable ally, and with a handful of troops courageous and gallant, but unaccustomed to the fatigues of long or disastrous campaigns; he undertook to march over the Alps and Apennines, to the extremity of Italy, through the dominions of the pope and Florence, who were openly declared against him.

After a number of delays and procrastinations, unavoidable at the commencement of such an enterprize, Charles began his march. While he waited at Ast in Piedmont for his artillery, which was obliged to be dragged over the mountains, he was seized with the small-pox; from which he recovered after the most imminent danger of his life. At Turin he was necessitated to borrow all the rings and jewels of the duchess of Savoy, as he did at Casal those of the marchioness of Montferrat, to supply the necessary charges of the war. Ludovico Sforza met him at Vigeve; but quitted him in a few days, to take poffeffion of the duchy of Milan, which he feized on the death of Galeazzo; his nephew, though he had left an infant fon. If Charles had purfued the dictates of found policy, he fhould himfelf have conquered Milan, which belonged of right to the family of Orleans; but, intoxicated with his Neapolitan fchemes, he continued his progrefs.

The Florentines, who paffionately afpired to freedom, expelled Pietro de Medecis on the king's approach to Tufcany; and received him in military triumph into the city. Clad in complete armour, mounted on horfeback, his lance couched, and his vizor lowered, he entered Florence as a conqueror. Alexander the fixth, the reigning pontiff, retired, at this tremendous intelligence, into the caftle of St. Angelo, after he had commanded the gates of Rome to be thrown open; and Charles, victorious without a blow, took poffeffion of the city as by right of conqueft, and difpofed poſed of his troops in the different quarters of it.—The pope ſoon capitulated; and after a treaty ſuch as the neceſſity of his affairs reduced him to conclude, the French army quitted Rome, and reſumed its march.— Meanwhile all was conſternation and affright at Naples. Alfonſo, who had ſucceeded to his father in the throne, yielding to terrors the moſt unmanly, and almoſt inconceivable, reſigned the ſceptre to young Ferdinand his ſon, and fled into a monaſtery at Meſſina in Sicily *. The new king

* If we may credit the hiſtorians, Alfonſo's panic roſe to a degree approaching frenzy. Such were his fears, that though the French army was ſixty leagues diſtant, he apprehended he ſaw them in the ſtreets of Naples, and that the very walls, trees, and ſtones, cried out, " France !" The queen-dowager imploring him only to remain three days, which were wanting to complete a year from his acceſſion to the crown, he refuſed; and even threatened, if he was longer detained againſt his inclination, to precipitate himſelf from the windows of the palace. After having cauſed his ſon Ferdinand to be ſolemnly crowned and inaugurated, he embarked on board a veſſel; carrying with him all ſorts of wines, and ſeeds for his gardens,

king was defeated in a fort of engagement which he hazarded, and obliged to fhelter himfelf in the ifle of Ifchia. Naples inftantly received the victor; the caftles held out a

gardens, to both which pleafures he was immoderately attached. Landing in Sicily, he retired into a convent at Meffina; and abandoning himfelf to fuperftitious and monaftic aufterities, foon contracted by thofe rigors an excoriation and gravel, which terminated his exiftence, within a year from Charles the eighth's invafion.

Cominés defcribes him as a monfter of impiety and cruelty. Some circumftances of his oppreffions and enormities, which he enumerates, are very fingular. " Both himfelf and his father Ferdinand," fays he, " were accuftomed to deliver out hogs to the people " to fatten, and if any of them died, they were " obliged to repay the king. He indulged himfelf in " the commiffion of every fpecies of lafcivioufnefs and " barbarity: fold the bifhopric of Tarento to a Jew " for thirteen thoufand ducats; and gave abbies to his " falconers." Cominés, with a fort of facred horror, fums up the lift of his iniquities, by declaring, that " he never kept Lent, or even pretended to do " it; and would neither go to confeffion, nor re-" ceive the facrament." Thefe were the moft flagitious exceffes of which the human mind could conceive an idea, in the fifteenth century, and feemed to eclipfe all his other vices.

very ſhort time; and of the whole kingdom, only Brindiſi continued to declare for Ferdinand.

Dazzled with ſo extraordinary a blaze of glory, Charles already meditated the ſack of Conſtantinople, and the ſubverſion of the Ottoman empire. Every thing yielded to his arms; and during ſo long and difficult a march, ſcarce an enemy had appeared to oppoſe his paſſage.—But amid this train of proſperity, he did not advert to the gathering ſtorm. Plunged in the feſtive exceſſes of youth, and fluſhed with conqueſt, no ſteps were taken to ſecure the dominions he had acquired. Banquets and maſquerades ſucceeded each other; and to ſo great a degree of neglect was their miſconduct carried, that troops were not even ſent to receive the places which ſubmitted, and acknowledged the French monarch.

The great powers of Europe, who had looked on, during this rapid ſubverſion of Italy, unmoved, began to awake from their ſupine inaction. A league was made between

between the pope, the emperor Maximilian, the archduke Philip his son, and Ferdinand of Arragon: even the perfidious Sforza, violating the ties of gratitude and honour, acceded to this powerful confederacy.

It became necessary for Charles to meditate a retreat. He determined on it, after having previously made a triumphal entry into the capital of his new kingdom, clad in the imperial ornaments, a globe in his right hand, and a sceptre in his left; while a canopy was supported over him by the first nobles of the country, and all the people cried, " Long live " the most august emperor !"—This ostentatious ceremony performed, he quitted Naples; and passing again through the papal territories, was so imprudent as to lose twelve or fifteen days at Pisa and Sienna, during which time the great confederate army assembled. Louis duke of Orleans, who ought to have led eight or nine thousand men to the assistance of his sovereign, had engaged in an attempt against

Ludovico

Ludovico Sforza; and having furprifed the city of Novarra, was afterwards blocked up in it.

The allied army, though four times more numerous than that of the king, did not venture to attack him among the mountains; but waited for him near the village of Fornoua, nine miles from Placenzia, in an open plain. The courage of the French, animated by the prefence of their prince, was fuperior to all oppofition: they gained the day, purfued their march towards France, and reached the city of Aft with laurels unwithered.—The duke of Orleans continued ftill fhut up in Novarra; but Charles at length marching to his relief, extricated him with difficulty from his perilous fituation, the garrifon having fuftained the extremeft preffures of famine.

The king had not fufficient patience to attend the conclufion of a treaty in agitation with Sforza; but, quitting the fatigues of a camp, returned in hafte to Lyons, and once more abandoned himfelf self to love and pleasures. All the hasty and imperfect trophies he had acquired, were soon forgotten. A decay in the affairs of Naples, as rapid as the conquest of it, rendered abortive all his labours. Ferdinand, more worthy of a diadem than his father or grandfather, returned to the kingdom from which he had been driven. The duke of Montpensier, left viceroy, after a long and obstinate attempt to retain possession of it, was not only obliged to surrender himself and his troops prisoners of war, but to capitulate for the complete evacuation of the whole kingdom in a month: and the other commanders refusing to acknowledge or execute so ignominious a treaty, he was sent, together with the forces which he commanded, to Puzzoli; where a malignant distemper destroyed both himself and the greater part of his unhappy countrymen. Ferdinand, a prince of high expectations, died likewise at this critical juncture, before the reduction of his dominions was effected;

fected; and his uncle Frederic succeeded to the throne *.

Meanwhile new plans of invasion were set on foot in the court of France. The king, in compliance with the superstition of the age, went to St. Denis, to take leave of the holy saints and martyrs who repose there. The cavalry even passed the mountains, and the duchy of Milan was fixed for the scene of their first attack; when all these preparations were suddenly stopt and laid aside. It is pretended, that Charles's attachment to one of the queen's maids of honour, occasioned this extraordinary change: but it is more natural to attribute it to the decay of his health; which, impaired by his excesses with women, and

---

* Ferdinand had only just married his own aunt, a beautiful young lady of fourteen years, as Cominés assures us. She was the legitimate daughter of his grandfather Ferdinand, and of consequence sister to the late king Alfonso, his father. He expired of a dysentery and hectic fever, in a little town at the foot of mount Vesuvius.

originally

originally delicate, began to fail. The duke of Orleans was so sensible of this apparent decline, which left the succession open to him, that he refused to take upon him the command of the army destined against Milan; and every appearance of war was totally relinquished.

The king, whether conscious that his pleasures had been productive of very injurious consequences to him; or whether, from motives of conscientious scruple, renounced all his past irregularities; and retiring with the queen, to whom he was exceedingly attached, to the castle of Amboise, amused himself with making some additions, and erecting new apartments there. Resigning the ideas of foreign conquest, he began to provide for the internal tranquillity of his kingdom; and was occupied in these regulations, when a death equally sudden and singular, put an end to his intentions.

He was in an old gallery at Amboise, from whence he surveyed a game of tennis, which

which was played in the foffes of the caf-tle. Willing to gratify the queen with the fame entertainment, he went to her chamber, and taking her by the hand, conducted her to the gallery; but in paffing through the door which opened into it, he ftruck his head with violence againft the top, which was very low : he felt no immediate bad confequences from the accident, but entered. He even had entirely forgotten the blow, and was engaged in deep converfation with Jacques de Refli, bifhop of Angers. It turned on religious fubjects; and the king, who had entirely renounced the debauches in which he had indulged during the firft years of his marriage, was profeffing his determined refolutions to guard facredly the fidelity he owed to the queen, when he fuddenly fell backwards in an apopleètic fit. The courtiers and attendants, terrified at fo alarming a feizure, immediately laid him on a fmall pallet-bed, which by accident was in a corner of the gallery; and on which, notwithftanding withstanding every effort of medicine, he expired at eleven o'clock the same night *.

The instant he had breathed his last, every one quitted his body; and leaving him in the place where he died, galloped in haste to Blois, to announce to the duke of Orleans his accession to the crown: while Anne of Bretagne, overcome with grief, and very strongly attached to her husband, abandoned herself to all the distraction of sorrow. It is said she sat in

* Philip de Cominés says, the king thrice recovered his voice, but quickly lost it again, as the confessor who waited by his majesty assured him. He calls the distemper of which Charles expired, a catarrh or apoplexy; and adds, that the indications of his approaching end were apparent to the physicians for three or four days before his seizure. Yet they entertained hopes that the disease would only fall on his arms, of which he would probably lose the use. Some of the French historians have notwithstanding pretended, though without any shadow of proof, or probability, that he was poisoned with an orange. It is more natural to apprehend that his irregularities enfeebled his constitution, and accelerated his end.

a corner

a corner of her chamber during two days, conſtantly refuſing any nouriſhment, and loſt in deſpair. Perhaps her mortified ambition might, in ſome degree, cauſe ſo immoderate a diſtreſs; as by Charles's death ſhe ſaw herſelf again reduced from queen of France to ducheſs of Bretagne; the two ſons which ſhe had borne him having both lived a very ſhort time.

The ſtrokes of Charles's character are few and ſimple. He was ſurnamed the Affable and the Courteous; nor is it known that in his whole life, he ever offended or diſguſted any one of his ſervants or ſubjects. His temper was ſweet, and yielding to exceſs; open to generoſity, humanity, and benevolence. — In perſon he was little, and ungraceful; his ſhoulders high, his face plain, and his ſpeech ſlow and interrupted *: his eyes alone were lively and expreſſive. Cominés's deſcription

---

* Brantome takes ſome pains to contradict this idea of Charles the eighth, and even produces the teſtimony of his grandmother, the ſenechale of Poictou, who

tion of him is wondroufly forcible, though laconic.—" Petit homme de corps, et peu " entendu; mais fi bon, qu'il n'eft point " poffible de voir meilleure créature."— There is a certain unadorned naiveté in the picture, which charms and affects.

Though Charles's paffion for women was exceffive, and is even fuppofed to have conduced to haften his death; yet we do not find any particular miftrefs who appears to have attached him long, or obtained any extraordinary afcendency

who had been a lady of honour under the duchefs of Bourbon (Anne de Beaujeu) and confequently knew the king's perfon perfectly. She defcribed him as having a handfome and engaging face, and though low and flender in his perfon, yet well made and agreeable.

If the effigy in bronze at St. Denis, where he is in a kneeling attitude, may be fuppofed to refemble the king, it confirms Brantome's affertion; who accufes Guichiardini of malignancy, in belying and depreciating his perfon, in revenge for the calamities he had introduced into Italy. Francis the firft cherifhed a peculiar veneration for, and affection to the memory of Charles the eighth.

over

over him. His capacity was limited, and rendered more so by the mean and confined education which he received in the castle of Amboise during his father's life; but the virtues of his heart, his observance of justice, and unbounded benignity of disposition, rendered him the most amiable of princes. Two of his domestics are said to have died of grief for the loss of their beloved master. He had not completed his twenty-eighth year, when death deprived his people of so good a king.

In him ended the direct race of Valois; Louis duke of Orleans, who ascended the throne, being of a collateral branch, and grandson to the first duke of Orleans, brother to Charles the sixth, assassinated in the rue Barbette at Paris.

CHAPTER THE FIFTH.

Louis the twelfth's accession and character.— His divorce, and marriage with Anne of Bretagne.—Conquest of Milan, and imprisonment of Ludovico Sforza.—Recovery of Naples, and division of it with Ferdinand of Arragon—Perfidy of that prince. —Gonsalvo de Cordova drives out the French.—Magnanimity of Louis.—His dangerous illness.—Death of Isabella of Castile.—Julius the second's accession to the papacy.—Character.—League of Cambray.—Death of the cardinal of Amboise. —Julius's ambition and successes.—Gaston de Foix appears.—His victories.—Battle of Ravenna.—Death—Circumstances.— French driven out of Italy.—Julius dies. —Leo the tenth accedes to the pontificate. —Illness and death of Anne of Bretagne.—Her character.—The king's grief. Marriage of Francis count d'Angoulesme to the princess Claude.—State of the court.—

Louis's marriage.— Illnefs. — Death.—Character.

LOUIS the twelfth had attained his thirty-fixth year at the time when he acceded to the crown of France. His judgment, naturally clear and difcerning, was ripened by experience; and his heart, full of every gentle and beneficent fentiment, was rendered fupremely capable of feeling the calamities of others, by thofe which he had undergone himfelf. Under Louis the eleventh he had been treated with cruel and unmerited feverity, compelled to a marriage the moft odious, and denied all the privileges of his rank. Under the fucceding regency, fortune perfecuted him with even greater rigour; and the error he committed in appearing in arms againft his fovereign at the battle of St. Aubin du Cormier, was fully expiated by a long and rigorous imprifonment, which fucceeded. The forgiving and clement temper of Charles the eighth had releafed him from this captivity, but he he was notwithstanding ever regarded with a sort of jealous attention; and was in disgrace with the late king at the time of his decease, on account of an unintended affront which Anne of Bretagne resented highly *.

The first acts of his administration were consistent with his character, and unveiled fully that virtuous integrity, and magnanimous superiority to revenge and retaliation of injury, which uniformly ap-

---

* The nature of this undesigned injury was very extraordinary. The young dauphin Charles was dead; and the physicians finding that the king's mind was much affected by so melancholy an event, advised some recreation to divert his grief, which might otherwise prey on his feeble constitution. The duke of Orleans, in this design, appeared at a masquerade in the castle of Amboise; and exerted himself to an unusual degree, in a dance, with a lady, which he carried to a pitch of gay extravagance. It produced the very opposite effect to that which he expected; for the queen interpreting all these marks of levity and mirth to his pleasure at the dauphin's death, which rendered him again presumptive successor, was exceedingly offended, and obliged him to leave the court, and retire to the castle of Blois.

peared

peared in his conduct. He lightened the impofts from off his people; and when preffed by the courtiers to punifh thofe who had been his enemies and avowed opponents, he made that glorious reply worthy of eternal remembrance; " It be-
" comes not a king of France, to revenge
" the quarrels of a duke of Orleans."

Though bent to recover the kingdom of Naples from Frederick the new fovereign, and equally determined to affert his title to the duchy of Milan, ufurped by Ludovico Sforza; a domeftic concern, which entailed with it very important confequences, claimed his early attention. The princefs Jane, to whom he had been married more than twenty years, though endowed with the moft eftimable and amiable qualities, was not only incapable of producing children; but the deformity of her perfon rendered her an object of diftafte and averfion. On the other hand, Anne of Bretagne had retired into her duchy; and though the articles of her marriage with Charles the eighth, were such as precluded her from the disposal of her hand in case of his death, to the injury of the state; yet policy required the strictest regard to those measures which might secure to the crown so rich an acquisition. She was beautiful in her person, though a little lame in one foot; yet in early youth, and had not only been beloved by Louis during the lifetime of her father Francis the second, but it was supposed had not been insensible to, or unaffected by his passion. These conjoined motives of the monarch and the man, induced Louis to apply to Alexander the sixth for a dissolution of his marriage: and the pope, whom political principles rendered subservient to any purposes or views, immediately appointed commissioners, and sent his son Cæsar Borgia into France, to decide the affair. They pronounced the union void and illegal, as having been effected by force: and the king, hastening to Nantes, at which city Anne resided, espoused her solemnly, and conducted her to Blois, where he commonly

monly held his court. Jane, submissive in her disgrace, and humble from a consciousness of her personal demerits, scarce attempted any resistance to the mandate which deprived her of a crown; but retiring to Bourges, devoted her remaining days to piety, and having founded an order of monastic seclusion, took the veil in the nunnery she had erected.

This affair transacted, the king directed his whole attention to Italy, and principally to the Milaneze. His claim was incontrovertible, in right of Valentina his grandmother; and this was rendered more apparent by the crimes and usurpation of Ludovico Sforza. After having concluded an alliance with the Venetians, his forces entered Piedmont; and meeting scarce any resistance, made a rapid conquest of the whole duchy, only the castle of Milan holding out a few days. Louis, on this prosperous intelligence, hastened acrofs the mountains, entered the capital of his new dominions habited in the ducal robes, and remained there near three months.

Sforza,

Sforza, who bent beneath the storm, and had early retired into Germany, waited only the favourable moment to return; at his approach, every city opened to him its gates, and he was received again into Milan, from whence he had fled. This faint gleam of succefs was quickly followed by a sad reverfe. The Switzers whom he entertained in his fervice, by a perfidy which even Sforza's character could not juftify, delivered him up to the French general, difguifed as a common foldier, under which appearance he had hoped to effect his efcape. He was conducted to Lyons, where Louis then refided: but Sforza's repeated and flagitious enormities had steeled his bofom to the impreffions of commiferation or pardon; and without deigning to admit him to his prefence, the king removed him immediately to the caftle of Loches in Touraine. At firft, his confinement was very rigorous, and it is pretended, that he was fhut up in an iron cage; but during the latter years of his life, this feverity was mitigated; he had permiffion to hunt, and a degree of liberty allowed him.

The complete reduction of all the Milaneze which followed Sforza's captivity, and the terror which Louis's arms spread through Italy, rendered the conqueſt of Naples almoſt certain: but his weakneſs in admitting Ferdinand the catholic to divide the ſpoils which he might have entirely appropriated, was eventually ſubverſive of all his acquiſitions. Previous to the attack, a convention was made between the two princes, by which Naples and the northern half of the kingdom was aſſigned to France; Ferdinand had Apulia and Calabria. Frederic, the reigning king, made no abler defence than his predeceſſors: after a timid and irreſolute oppoſition, finding himſelf reduced from royalty to the condition of an individual; and abandoned by all his ſubjects or adherents, he took the reſolution to throw himſelf on Louis's bounty. He demanded a ſafe conduct into France, which was granted him; and the king, with that generoſity which

eminently

eminently shone in his conduct, afforded him an asylum, and an annual pension of thirty thousand ecus, which was continued even after the expulsion of the French from Naples.

Meanwhile Ferdinand was not less diligent in securing his share of the Neapolitan territories. Gonsalvo de Cordova, the celebrated general, whom history has dignified with the title of " the Great Cap-" tain," made an easy conquest of the two provinces decreed to his master. Tarentum only made resistance. Alfonso, the heir to the crown, and son of Frederic, was shut up in it. His father, supposing it impregnable, had sent him to this fortress under the care of two nobles attached to his interests: they apprehending every thing lost, and reposing on the solemn promises of Gonsalvo, who swore on the sacraments, to leave the young prince his perfect liberty, capitulated, and surrendered the place: but the perfidious Spaniard, who sported with oaths, and disregarded the most binding compacts, detained Alfonso prisoner,

prisoner, and sent him to Ferdinand, who though he treated him with lenity, never would release him.

Scarce was Naples reduced under its new masters, when dissentions arose between them, on the subject of a small tract of country claimed by both. The Spaniards first infringed the peace by acts of open hostility; but the king having commanded to repel force by force, his general the duke of Nemours took the field, and pushed his advantages over the Spaniard to such a length, that he was reduced to retire into Barletta, where the want of ammunition had nearly compelled him to surrender. At this juncture, when Louis was on the point of dispossessing Ferdinand of all his division, and fortune had uniformly attended on his arms, Philip the archduke, who had married Jane the daughter of Ferdinand and Isabel, passed through France: he saw the king at Lyons, and concluded a treaty with him in the name of his father-in-law. By the conditions of it, the two monarchs were

bound

bound to a ceſſation of arms; the provinces originally ceded to each were confirmed, and the lands in diſpute were to be ſequeſtered into the hands of the archduke.

In the conduct of the princes after this event, we trace in the ſtrongeſt manner their oppoſite genius and character. The ambaſſadors of Ferdinand who attended Philip, having ſworn to the execution of the agreement, under pain of excommunication if violated or infringed, the heralds announced it to the two commanders in Naples. The duke of Nemours, who knew the uprightneſs and integrity of his king, heſitated not a moment to withdraw his forces : but Gonſalvo, hardened himſelf to the commiſſion of crimes, and repoſing with full ſecurity on the baſe and treacherous perfidy of Ferdinand, refuſed to act in compliance with the orders; he demanded an expreſs command to that purpoſe. Having received a reinforcement of Germans, he in turn attacked the French, routed them in two actions, killed the duke of Nemours, and not only

made

made himſelf maſter of the city of Naples, but totally ſubdued the whole kingdom.

The archduke was in Savoy when he received the news of ſo notorious a breach of that public faith, for which he had pledged his own honour. Shocked at a conduct which marked its author with indelible infamy, he returned inſtantly into France to put himſelf into Louis's power; while he diſpatched meſſengers to remonſtrate with his father-in-law on his treacherous connivance and approval of Gonſalvo's miſconduct, and demanded the reſtitution of all he had conquered. Ferdinand, wrapping himſelf in the duplicity of an equivocating and crooked policy, one time diſowned his ambaſſadors, and at another his general; offered to reſtore the kingdom to the captive Frederic, but ſecretly ſent orders to puſh the war in Naples to the abſolute extermination of the French.

Louis, great in his own virtue, and ſcorning theſe deſpicable ſubterfuges, ordered the miniſters of the king of Arragon

gon to quit his dominions; and while, incapable himfelf of mean retaliation, he permitted the archduke, unmolefted, to return into Flanders, though he might have detained him, he made that animating fpeech to him at his departure.—" If," faid he, " your father-in-law has been " guilty of a perfidy, I will not refemble " him; and I am infinitely happier in " the lofs of a kingdom which I know " how to reconquer, than to have ftained " my honour, which I could never re-" trieve."

Irritated by a treatment fo unkingly and deteftable, Louis made new, but ineffectual efforts to regain his rights in Naples. Gonfalvo, the ableft commander of his age, defeated all his attempts; and retained by military fkill and fuperior parts, the poffeffions which he had acquired by a breach of every principle of faith.

The death of Alexander the fixth, and the acceffion of Julius the fecond to the pontificate, was likewife unfavourable to the affairs of France; and the ill fuccefs which

which from every quarter seemed to overwhelm him, threw the king into a violent fever, produced by anxiety and mortification. During the heighth of his distemper, as his death was apprehended to be imminent and inevitable, Anne of Bretagne, provident for her own safety, began to prepare for a retreat into her duchy; and in that intention, embarked a number of rich moveables in boats upon the Loire. The marechal de Gié meeting them between Saumur and Nantes, gave orders to stop their progress; thinking it an act contradictory to the interests of the state, that the queen should remove at pleasure all her jewels and effects out of the kingdom.——Louis recovered; and Anne, enraged at what she deemed an action of the most presumptuous insolence, vindictive to excess, and in a capacity to revenge severely the marechal's conduct, not only procured his exile from the court, and deprivation of every post he held; but pushing her vengeance to a length the most unjustifiable and cruel,

reduced

reduced him to extreme poverty, and left him to terminate his miserable days amid disgrace and indigence.

Frederic, the unfortunate king of Naples, expired about this time at Tours, in a mild and honourable captivity. His death was followed by that of the great queen of Castile, Isabella; and her dominions devolving to the archduke Philip in right of Jane his wife, changed the whole scale and system of European politics. Ferdinand, who after several vain and fruitless efforts to retain the regency, was again reduced to his original kingdom of Arragon, reconciled himself with the king of France; and married his niece Germana de Foix, in hopes of issue which might exclude his grandchildren from the possession of the two thrones.

Julius the second's character, who had ascended the papal chair, though less flagitious than that of his predecessor, was not less opposite to the genius of that religion under which he held the highest place. Haughty, ambitious, warlike, splendid,

did, and enterprizing, nature had defigned him for the helmet, not the tiara, and formed him to fhine in camps, rather than in conclaves. Politically ungrateful, and finking the prieft and the individual in the prince, he forgot the protection which Louis had extended to him under Alexander's pontificate, when he found a refuge from his generofity. Jealous of his retaining a power in Italy which, might be fatal to the little potentates among whom it was divided, he exerted all the powers of his turbulent and reftlefs genius, in exciting enemies to the French; and unreftrained either by the fanctity of his character, or advanced period of life, he did not fcruple to appear in arms, and lead on his troops in perfon.

The archduke Philip's fudden and unexpected death again reftored to Ferdinand the adminiftration he had loft. As he was in Italy when this event happened, an interview took place at Savona between him and Louis the twelfth. The former's terrors left the king of France
fhould

should oppose his designs on the regency of Castile, was his concealed motive to it. They again renewed their alliance, and swore to the strict observance of the articles of peace; but Ferdinand, who knew no principle of public or private fidelity, and only sacrificed to his interested views, disregarded and violated every condition on his return into Spain.

The great league of Cambray followed soon after. One cannot but consider with astonishment mingled with indignation, an union of the two greatest kings in Europe, the emperor, and the pope, against a small, though opulent republic. Louis was guilty of a still greater error, in allying himself with his three inveterate and natural enemies, Ferdinand, Maximilian, and Julius, against the Venetians, his only sure and firm ally beyond the mountains. The battle of Ghiera-d'Adda, gained over Alviano their general, reduced the state to the verge of ruin; and had the emperor improved the deplorable circumstances of their

their defeat with celerity, Venice herself had probably been fwallowed up by this prodigious confederacy. She averted the final blow, but could never retrieve her former luftre or extent of territory; and Louis, who was rather influenced by refentment than political motives in this affair, had but too much reafon to repent the error he had committed, during the future part of his reign.

The death of the cardinal of Amboife, firft minifter of ftate, was another lofs to the kingdom. He was one of the moft virtuous and difinterefted ftatefmen, of whom any hiftory has made mention. Equally a ftranger to pride and to avarice; a cardinal, with only one ecclefiaftical benefice, and folely occupied by the interefts of his fovereign and his country, he was lamented with their grateful tears.

Julius the fecond, bent on the aggrandizement of the papacy, and the expulfion of the French from Italy, no longer obferved any meafures with Louis: while the king, actuated by fcruples of a timid fuperftition,

KINGS OF FRANCE, &c. 163

superstition, forbad his generals to make incursions on the lands of the church, and spared the pontiff from reverence to his character. Emboldened by this treatment, he proceeded to the greatest lengths of tyranny and inordinate ambition. Desirous of annexing Ferrara to the patrimony of St. Peter, he ordered his general to lay siege to Mirandola, though in the midst of a most severe winter, and though by no shadow of equity could he justify the attempt. The advances not being made with that rapidity he expected, he repaired thither himself; appeared in the trenches at seventy years of age, encouraged and exhorted his troops to the attack; and on its surrender, caused himself to be carried into the city in military triumph, through the breach in the wall.

Roused by these acts of violence and hostility, the king at length sent orders to Chamont to spare the pope no longer. The commander, in consequence, pressed his holiness so vigorously, that he obliged him to retire to Ravenna; and would have

have compelled him to terms of pacification, had he not been feized at this juncture with a mortal diftemper. Touched with horror at the crime he had committed in bearing arms againſt the holy father; and yielding under the preſſures of approaching death, to all the weakneſs of abjeɛt fuperſtition, he ſent to implore his forgiveneſs and abfolution. The operations of war ſtood ſtill, and Julius had time to recover. Fortune, which was not fo favourable to him as the influence of religious prejudice, foon however reduced him again to a fituation the moſt perilous and critical: he apprehended his degradation from the papacy; and faw Rome itſelf expofed to the army of the king, without any capacity of defence. He was even on the verge of recurring to Louis's generofity, and opening a treaty with him; when having received advice, that, tired with the fcruples and importunities of the queen, he had forbid his general to attack the territories of the church; he refumed his wonted haughtineſs,

nefs, revoked his intentions of peace, and prepared himself for new campaigns.

In this century, when the minds of men, cultivated and enlarged by learning, expanded by philofophy, and divefted of prejudice or the flavery of prefcription, prefume to view objects as they are by the fteady light of reafon; we are amazed at the weaknefs of our anceftors: and furvey with mingled wonder and indignation, an Alexander or a Julius, revered amid a thoufand enormities; and exerting a tyrannical fway over the cabinets of princes, or conduct of generals, by the fole terrors of their facerdotal office, unaccompanied with any virtues, or even the appearances of morality and decorum.

Unrepreffed by age and ill fuccefs, the pope meditated frefh fchemes of conqueft. Louis, the virtuous, the merciful, and the good, was the conftant object of his animofity. He entered into an alliance with Ferdinand the moft faithlefs of princes, againft him; and Venice acceded to the league, which was named by a mockery of religion, "the holy." They took Brefcia, and befieged Bologna—when Gafton de Foix appeared. This young hero, nephew to the king, had fcarce attained his twentieth year. Louis fondly loved him; and difcerning all the fire of military genius in him, entrufted to his fupreme command the army in Italy. His firft exploits not only juftified the choice his uncle made, but elevated him to a rank above all the captains of his age. During the heighth of the fiege of Bologna, he entered the city amid a prodigious fall of fnow unperceived by the affailants, who covered with confufion, inftantly retired from before it. He loft not a moment in pufhing his advantage; defeated the Venetian commander who oppofed his march towards Brefcia; and attacking their entrenchments with only fix thoufand chofen foldiers, put eight thoufand of the enemy to the fword, and totally drove them from the furrounding country. Thefe fplendid fucceffes were

foon

soon followed by the great battle of Ravenna. Gaston triumphed over the army of the confederates; but, like Gustavus Adolphus, he expired in the arms of victory. His own ardour and youthful impetuosity of valour were the causes of his lamented death. Desirous to render the glory of the day complete, he pursued with a small troop, a body of four thousand Spaniards, who retreated in good order. They surrounded him; and he was killed after having combated with the most heroic courage, pierced with twenty-two wounds. The Italians regarded him as a prodigy, and he was surnamed " the thun-
" der-bolt of Italy," from the violence of his movement, the rapidity of his progress, and the suddenness of his extinction *.

Louis

* Brantome enumerates several minute circumstances, preceding and accompanying his death. The action was already gained, when the celebrated Chevalier Bayard, seeing the young prince covered with the blood and brains of a soldier who had been killed close to him, rode up, and demanded, if he was wounded? " No," replied Gaston, " but I have
" wounded

MEMOIRS OF THE

Louis was greatly affected at his nephew's untimely fate; and the sequel proved

" wounded many of the enemy." Bayard implored him on no confideration to quit the main body of the army; and to prevent his troops from pillaging, while he purfued himfelf the flying fquadrons. This wholefome and wife advice was overborn by the young hero's martial fury. A Gafcon runaway having informed him, that a body of Spaniards not only maintained their ground, but had repulfed fome of his own forces; he inftantly charged them in perfon, crying out, " Who loves me, follows me."—This body of veterans were advantageoufly pofted, near a piece of water: they difcharged their harquebuffes, and then lowering their pikes, received firmly the attack. Gafton's horfe was firft killed, and he himfelf overborn by numbers; only about twenty gentlemen had accompanied him, among whom was Lautrec, afterwards fo renowned under Francis the firft, in the wars of Italy. He was of the houfe of Foix, and nearly allied by blood to Gafton, whom he defended with the moft heroic bravery—crying out, when no longer able to ward off the blows aimed at him, " Spare the general, brother to your " queen Germana, and you fhall have immenfe ran- " fom !"— No exclamations or intreaties could however fave the prince; and Lautrec himfelf fell by his fide, covered with wounds, and left upon the plain

as

proved how much the affairs of war depend on one man. The animating spirit which diffused life and vigour, was extinct: diffentions arose in the victorious army, no longer united under one great chieftain. Julius, who overcome with difmay, was ready to implore the clemency of the king, was re-encouraged by Ferdinand and the Venetians. A feries of difaftrous circumftances fucceeded each other, and ruined the French affairs: inftead of giving law to all Italy, as might have been expected, they experienced a fad reverfe.

The Switzers breaking in upon the Milanefe, almoft deftitute of defence, reconquered it, after a fubjection of twelve years, and replaced Maximilian Sforza in the duchy. Genoa revolted, and created

---

as dead. Bayard was almoft driven to madnefs when on his return he learned his general's fate: and into fo great a confternation were the French thrown by this unexpected difafter, that, had the enemy rallied and returned to the charge, they would infallibly have been defeated.

a new

a new duke. Henry the eighth of England, excited by the artifices of his father-in-law Ferdinand, sent to declare war against France; and Maximilian basely deserting all his engagements, went over to the opposite party, and even formed a new alliance with the pope. The king of Arragon, improving the opportunity which this union of so many powers afforded him against Louis, attacked the little kingdom of Navarre, and soon reduced it to subjection. Superior force, and a bull of Julius posterior to the conquest, were the only pretexts which Ferdinand could employ, for this cruel outrage on a prince unarmed, and who had never rendered himself obnoxious to his displeasure. The king of France made every effort to replace him on the throne, and even sent an army into Navarre, but without success: he was engaged with too many enemies, who attempted to overpower him on all hands.

The death of Julius seemed to promise better fortune in Italy. Leo the tenth, a name a name renowned in arts and liberal science, opened his short, but memorable reign. New efforts were made upon the Milanese in alliance with the Venetians. Sforza was driven to the last extremities by the French forces; only Como and Novarra persisted to hold out—but all these laurels withered in less time than they had been gathered; and after the loss of an engagement, where all the Gascon infantry was hewn in pieces, scarce could la Tremouille, wounded in the leg, conduct the cavalry in safety back to Savoy.

Meanwhile, Henry and Maximilian uniting against Louis, joined to attack Picardy; and the Switzers, elate with the advantages they had gained, entered Burgundy, and laid siege to Dijon, with two-and-twenty thousand men. By means of a treaty humiliating though necessary to France, these latter enemies were induced to return into their own country; but the king of England and the emperor gained the battle of Guinegate, took Tournay, and

and spread terror through all the neighbouring provinces. Louis, though shaken by such a concurrence of calamitous accidents, supported with magnanimity the shock: but wearied by the supplications of the queen, and hoping that Leo might aid his arms which he had hitherto opposed, he sent two prelates to make his submissions to the see of Rome, and to testify his contrition and penitence for his past offences. This act, which may be intirely attributed to the influence of Anne of Bretagne over his mind, was the last of her life. She died at the castle of Blois, of a distemper caused by the improper treatment she received in her last lying-in, and only thirty-seven years of age.

The French historians, biassed by the dowry which she brought to the kingdom, have exhausted themselves in panegyrics on this princess. Her piety, her chastity, her liberality, her attachment to the two successive kings her husbands; her capacity, and spirit, have all been subjects of eulogium. Imaginary and ideal qualities
have

have been added to complete the picture. I muſt confeſs, her conduct as a queen does not appear to juſtify theſe extravagant encomiums. Force and neceſſity alone reduced her to give her hand to Charles the eighth; nor though blameleſs as a wife, did ſhe ever love the people or country over which ſhe reigned. On the contrary, ſhe ever cheriſhed the moſt avowed predilection for the houſe of Auſtria; and endeavoured by every exertion of addreſs or perſuaſion, to induce the king to marry his eldeſt daughter Claude to the young archduke, who was afterwards Charles the fifth. Diſappointed in this intention by Louis's better principles, and attentive regard to France, ſhe attempted to transfer the ſucceſſion of Bretagne to her youngeſt daughter, and to marry her to the ſame prince. Though both theſe ſchemes, ſo big with ruinous conſequences, were rendered abortive; ſhe yet had ſufficient influence over Louis, to retard and even totally prevent during her life, the conſummation of the princeſs
Claude's

Claude's nuptials with Francis count d'Angoulême, to whom the united voice of the nation had deftined her, as prefumptive heir of the crown: and her death, which only preceded that of the king by a fingle year, may be regarded as happy to the ftate, in every point of view. Her bigotted veneration, and blind fubmiffion to popes or priefts, was highly detrimental to the king's affairs; whofe fucceffes were always checked in the midway, by her import unateentreaties in their favour. Unforgiving and vindictive, fhe never pardoned an injury, or knew any limits to her refentment of it. Notwithftanding thefe inconteftable defects, fhe was infinitely dear to her hufband, who was during fome time inconfolable for her lofs. He remained feveral days fhut up in his chamber, entirely devoted to grief; ordered all the comedians or muficians to quit the court, and refufed audience to every minifter or ambaffador who did not appear in deep mourning. Yielding however to motives of public good, which

eyer

ever formed the line of his actions, he conferred his eldest daughter on the count d'Angoulesme; and the nuptials were solemnized at St. Germain-en Laye *.

The death of the queen, together with Francis's marriage, gave a new face to affairs. Louisa of Savoy, mother to the heir of the crown, began to display her shining, but dangerous character: and Louis, grown wise by experience, tender of his people, and frugal of the revenues, viewed with a melancholy foresight, the profusion and expensive munificence, which the count d'Angoulesme's character pre-

* Several conjoined motives, not totally void of weight, privately considered, rendered Anne of Bretagne peculiarly averse to this union.—She always flattered herself with hopes of male issue by the king. She detested madame Louisa, Francis's mother, whose unsubmitting spirit never bent beneath her. Above all, she feared and foresaw her child's unhappy days with Francis. This was too much verified in the result. She was by no means beautiful; and her husband, amorous and inconstant, never loved her: and if he treated her with respect himself, could not, or did not exact the same behaviour from his mother.

dicted;

dicted. In this anticipation of the evils which such qualities would probably entail on his kingdom, he used frequently to exclaim, "Ce gros gars-la gatera tout!" It is even highly to be suspected, that this formed one of the great motives to his third marriage; though the desire of effecting a close union and alliance with England, formed a more ostensible pretext.

Henry the eighth had a sister of uncommon beauty. The duke de Longueville, who had been taken prisoner at the battle of Guinegate, being sent over to negotiate a treaty of peace, first opened the overtures for this match, which were immediately accepted. The princess was conducted into France; received at Boulogne by a splendid train, at the head of which was the count d'Angoulesme, and married at Abbeville to the king. She was in early youth, gay, and fond of pleasure: her heart, susceptible of the impressions of tenderness and passion, had already engaged itself to a young English lord,

whom

whom Henry had created duke of Suffolk, and to whom he had even intended to give his fifter's hand. Under thefe circumftances, it cannot be fuppofed that Louis, a valetudinarian finking into years, worn by the fatigues of war, tormented with the gout, and occupied continually with the recollection of his late queen, could be a very acceptable hufband. Francis, amorous and gallant to excefs, was captivated with her charms : and it is pretended that he might and would have pufhed his good fortune to the utmoft length; if political confiderations, and his mother's reprehenfions, had not, though with difficulty, impofed a reftraint on his defires *.

Meanwhile

* I find it impoffible not to enter a little into this ftory, curious and interefting in itfelf, and on which the French writers have been very inquifitive and diffufe. Moft of the cotemporary authors relate very circumftantially an anecdote, which, if true, puts it beyond all doubt, that Francis had gained the moft complete and tender intereft in the young queen's affections. Preffed by the importunities of her lover,

Meanwhile Louis touched the verge of life. His nuptial pleasures conducted him to

and yielding to his entreaties, she at length granted him a rendezvous in the palace of the Tournelles; and there can be little question that such an interview would have been decisive. The count habited himself in the most gallant manner, and was hastening to the queen's apartment, when he was met by Grignaux, an ancient gentleman who had been in the service of Anne of Bretagne. Struck with the more than common magnificence of his dress, knowing his predominant weakness, and mistrustful of his intentions, Grignaux rudely stopt him; and addressing him, demanded whither he was going so hastily. Francis refused to answer satisfactorily to this question—" Donnez vous en bien garde, Monseigneur," said he frowning; " pasques Dieu! vous vous jouez " à vous donner un maître; il ne faut qu'un accident " pour que vous restiez Comte d'Angoulesme toute " votre vie."—This bold and peremptory remonstrance was not lost on the person to whom it was directed. Francis paused on the very threshold of his mistress's chamber: love and empire disputed for an instant in his bosom. The latter triumphed; and submitting to Grignaux's counsel, he had either the magnanimity or the weakness to suffer himself to be led away from the temptation, and conducted out of the palace.

Notwithstanding

to the tomb. Forgetting his maxim which he ufed frequently to repeat, that " Love " is the king of young perfons, but the " tyrant of old men," he abandoned himfelf to his immoderate fondnefs for the new queen. His conftitution, already fhaken, and debilitated by a flow fever, could not long fuftain thefe unufual efforts. While elated with hope of future conquefts, and fecure on the fide of England, he determined again to attack the Milanefe, and prepared a confiderable army to pafs the Alps, he was feized

Notwithftanding the air of the marvellous fpread through this adventure, it muft be confeffed that there is nothing in it either unnatural or improbable. Brantome not only relates it, but adds, " that Mary at- " tempted to counterfeit pregnancy on the death of the " king." Madame Louifa was not to be fo over-reached, when a crown depended on the fact, and foon difcovered the deceit. To this laft part, however, no faith is due, nor does any other author affert it. Befides, it is univerfally allowed that fhe was exceedingly attached to Charles Brandon, duke of Suffolk. Her conduct towards him, and marriage, put this beyond a doubt. Scarce three months elapfed between Louis's death, and her fecond nuptials.

with a dyfentery at the palace of the Tournelles in Paris; which reduced him fo low, that he breathed his laft a few days after, at fifty-three years of age.

He was the moft virtuous prince that France ever faw reign; perhaps who has reigned in Europe. It was proclaimed in the hall of the palace at his death, "Le bon roi Louis douze, Pere du peuple, eft mort!"—The tears of forrow and commiferation which he ufed to fhed, when the neceffities of war or ftate obliged him to levy an additional fubfidy, however fmall, on his people, prove how juftly he merited the appellation of their parent. His clemency, his benevolence, and unbounded philanthropy, were not inferior to Henry the fourth's: nor were thefe benign qualities obfcured and diminifhed by that unhappy and frantic paffion for women, by thofe pernicious foibles which accompanied the founder of the houfe of Bourbon to the grave. He was himfelf a pattern of conjugal fidelity; and his court, decent and reftrained, neither

ther knew the elegant politenefs, or the luxurious gallantry, which Francis the firſt introduced on his acceffion to the throne. His valour and military capacity had been diſtinguiſhed in many campaigns. His temper open, candid, and chearful, made him eafy of accefs, and gracious to the higheſt degree. He loved letters, and protected their authors; but did not extend to them that princely liberality, which has immortalized his fucceffor. Through his whole character, we trace none of thofe fplendid and glittering vices, which in kings, are too apt to dazzle and even delight; which carry in them that delufive magic, fo calculated to impofe on the human mind. His encomiaſts were not poets and men of genius, prone to proſtitute their talents. The voice of a whole people, their fimple and unembelliſhed lamentations, were his beſt panegyric. His perfon refembled the mind which animated it. Not elegant or beautiful, but amiable, intereſting, and agreeable.

For his vices I fearch in vain. The ſhades

shades of his character I mean not to hide. His attachment to the queen sometimes degenerated into uxoriousness, and caused him to commit errors very injurious to his affairs. He was duped by Ferdinand, and insulted by Julius.—In him expired the elder branch of the house of Orleans, and that of Angoulesme succeeded.

CHAPTER

CHAPTER THE SIXTH.

Acceſſion and Character of Francis the firſt. —Character of Louiſa counteſs d'Angouleſme.—Battle of Marignano.—Death of Ferdinand of Arragon and the emperor Maximilian.—Interview of Francis and Henry the eighth.—Commencement of the wars between the king and emperor.— Character of Charles of Bourbon. — Of Bonnivet. — Death of Leo the tenth.— Milan loſt.—Execution of Semblençai.— Conſpiracy of the conſtable of Bourbon.— Minute circumſtances of his treaſon and flight.—Death of the Queen.—The admiral Bonnivet enters Italy.—Bourbon lays ſiege to Marſeilles.—Francis purſues him over the Alps.—Battle of Pavia.—Minute enumeration of the circumſtances of the king's impriſonment.—Death of Bonnivet.—Francis's confinement, and removal to Madrid.—Meaſures of the regent.— The king's rigorous captivity.—Illneſs.—

Viſit of the ducheſs of Alençon, his ſiſter. —Releaſe.—Entry into his dominions.— Commencement of the ducheſs of Eſtampes' favour.

THE acceſſion of Francis the firſt to the crown, was accompanied with all thoſe circumſtances which could diffuſe over it a particular luſtre. Nature had laviſhly endowed him with every quality of mind and perſon, formed to intoxicate both his people and himſelf. He had only paſſed his twentieth year a few months. Finely formed, with the mien and appearance of a hero, his bodily accompliſhments were not inferior to his external figure. He excelled in the exerciſes of a cavalier, and puſhed the lance with diſtinguiſhed vigour and addreſs. Courteous in his manners, bounteous in his temper even to prodigality; the nobility, whom Louis the twelfth's œconomical frugality, and more reſerved deportment, had kept at greater diſtance, crowded round their youthful ſovereign with mingled pleaſure fure and admiration. Eloquent in the cabinet, and courageous in the field, he fhone alike in arts or arms; and while he extended his generofity to fcience and genius, impatiently panted for the occafion of fignalizing his prowefs, and acquiring the glory of a warrior *.

The fituation of affairs at the death of the late king, gave immediate field to this martial fpirit. Francis, equally determined to conquer the Milanefe as his predeceffor had been, laid inftant and open claim to that duchy; nor did he either

---

* We may judge of the eclat with which Francis opened his reign, and how high was his reputation through all Europe, by the brilliant colours, with which Guichiardini has drawn his chara&er. The portrait is wondroufly flattering. — " Delle vir-
" tù, della magnanimità, dello ingegno, et fpirito
" generofo di coftui, s'haveva univerfalmente tanta
" fperanzza, che ciafcuno confeffava non effere gia
" per moltiffimi anni pervenuto alcuno, con maggiore
" efpettatione alla corona. Perche gli conciliava
" fomma gratia il fiore dell'eta, che era di 22 anni,
" la bellezza egregia del corpo, la liberalità grandif-
" fima, la humanita fomma con tutti, et la notitia
" piena di molte cofe."

withdraw

withdraw his pretenfions, or fufpend his preparations, in confequence of the formidable alliance, which Ferdinand, Maximilian, Sforza, the Switzers, and foon after Leo the tenth, formed for its prefervation. While he repaired himfelf to Lyons, a part of his army croffed the mountains. After having furmounted infinite difficulties in the carriage of the artillery over rocks and precipices, they effected their paffage; and ufed fuch extraordinary celerity as to furprize Profper Colonna, who lay encamped with a thoufand cavalry upon the Po, juft as he was about to fit down to table, totally unapprehenfive of their approach.

At this news, the king fet forward to join his forces; having firft deferred the regency during his abfence, to the countefs d'Angoulefme his mother. She acted too high and important a part under the reign of Francis, not to enter minutely into her character. She connected all the great qualities and defects of an elevated, but ill-regulated mind. The beauty of her
perfon

person was scarce exceeded by that of any woman in the court; and, like her son, she surpassed in all those accomplishments of body, which confer elegance and grace. During the years of retirement which she had spent at the castle of Cognac in Angoumois after her husband's death, the education of her son had constituted her sole occupation: and to her care on this important point, the nation was indebted for the greater part of those mature and manly qualifications which rendered their sovereign an object of love and homage.— Her ambition and thirst of power were in some measure justified by her talents for government. She possessed courage personal and political; a magnanimity of soul undepressed even in adversity; uncommon penetration, firmness, and capacity.—But these endowments were sullied and contrasted by yet superior faults. Not less vindictive than Anne of Bretagne, she trampled on public or private feelings of whatever nature, to gratify her resentment; and borne away by the impetuosity

of

of her paffions, abufed the influence which fhe poffeffed over the king, to purpofes the moft pernicious and criminal. Rapacious of the national treafures, and avaritious in the accumulation of her own; with all the little foibles of her fex, and a flave to more than female vanity; her bofom was yet fufceptible of, and open to, all that ftorm of violent and contradictory emotions, which love and jealoufy occafion in the human heart. Such was the celebrated Louifa of Savoy.

Meanwhile Francis having put himfelf at the head of his army, marched forward into the Milanefe. All the cities opened their gates to him without a blow; and the Switzers, uncertain whether to treat or give battle, retiring before him, he encamped at Marignano, only a league diftant from Milan. A reinforcement of ten thoufand men arriving to their aid, determined them to the latter; and actuated by a fort of military frenzy, which the exhortations of the cardinal of Sion had infpired, they came furioufly to attack

tack the French in their lines. Hiftory fcarce affords any inftance of an action, difputed with fo enraged an animofity. It began about four in the afternoon in the month of October, and lafted more than three hours after the night clofed in. Laffitude and darknefs interpofed a ceffation of arms, without diminifhing the ardour of the combatants, or deciding the fortune of the day; and fo intimately were they mingled during the heat of the conteft, that many fquadrons repofed among thofe of the enemy. Francis himfelf, after having difplayed the higheft intrepidity, laid himfelf down upon the carriage of a piece of artillery; and, like Darius after the battle of Arbela, is faid to have feized with eagernefs a little water mixed with dirt and blood, which one of his foldiers brought him in a cafque, to affuage his thirft. With the dawn of light, the Switzers renewed the charge; but at length were repulfed with prodigious carnage: and a part of them being cut to pieces in a wood where they attempted
to

to shelter themselves, the rest retreated in good order. Ten thousand remained upon the field.

The terror which this victory inspired, together with the return of the Swiss troops into their own country, left Sforza almost destitute of any assistance. He retired however into the castle of Milan, and endeavoured to defend himself in that fortress: but finding it impracticable, he surrendered it to the constable Charles of Bourbon, on honorary conditions; and a very ample pension being assigned him in France, was conducted into that kingdom. All the duchy immediately received the French.

This conquest was followed by an interview between Francis and Leo. It took place at Bologna. The artful pontiff flattered the young monarch, and dextrously bent him to the purposes he wished: their conference ended, the king returned in haste to Lyons, where his mother waited for him, and his arrival was signalized by acclamations of triumph.

Ferdinand king of Arragon expired at this time of a dropfy and atrophy, occafioned by the incentives which his queen Germana of Foix had adminiftered to him, in hopes of iffue. His own hereditary dominions, together with thofe of Ifabella, defcended to young Charles the archduke. This event did not prevent the emperor from making a great effort on Italy. He broke in upon the Milanefe with near forty thoufand Switzers and Germans, and even laid fiege to Milan : but the tardy irrefolution which ever characterized all Maximilian's enterprizes, giving time to the conftable to approach the city, though with inferior forces, he retired; and his troops ill paid, were with difficulty kept together, and at length difbanded.

If the perfonal character of Francis, and the uniform fuccefs which had hitherto attended on him, might with reafon give umbrage to the little powers of Italy; that of Charles was yet more alarming, as more ample and extenfive. To the united realms of Caftile and Arragon,
he

he joined Naples, the Netherlands, and the Indies; and fuperadded to thefe was the expectation of the imperial crown, which Maximilian's age and infirmities feemed to render near at hand. Francis himfelf forefaw the gathering ftorm, and attempted to diffipate or delay it by a treaty concluded at Montpelier, which was foon after followed by another with Henry the eighth of England: but the death of Maximilian broke down thefe infufficient barriers; and opening a field of competition fo important and uncommon, laid the bafis of private animofity and public wars, which though fometimes fufpended, were never terminated or adjufted, during the lives of the two rivals.

The emperor died at Lintz upon the Danube, while he was employed in attempts to gain the electoral fuffrages, for his grandfon's nomination as king of the Romans. Charles and Francis inftantly declared themfelves candidates for the empire, though without any external or apparent marks of mutual antipathy:

it was soon decided, and the fo.mer afcended the imperial throne.

This increafe of fplendour and of power yet farther alarmed the king; and his difappointed ambition confpiring with his political terrors, from the union of fo many ftates under one fovereign, conduced to haften an interview previoufly agreed on between him and Henry. It took place between Ardres and Guifnes in the month of June. A magnificence unequalled, and which refulted from the temper of the two princes, fplendid, profufe, and vain, made the fpot retain the name of " the field of the cloth of gold." It lafted ten or twelve days; tournaments, banquets, and every fpecies of diverfion were exhibited. The queens of either monarch honoured it with their prefence; and Francis expended in this empty fpectacle, ufelefs to his kingdom, a greater fum than Charles had diftributed to acquire the imperial crown. It was attended with no durable or folid friendfhip between the kings. By a ftroke of policy without éclat, but more fage and effectual, the young emperor had paffed into England previous to the vifit; and entered into connections with Henry, which experience proved to be much more permanent and binding.

While the ceremony of Charles's coronation was performed at Aix-la-Chapelle, Francis made an unfuccefsful effort to reconquer the little kingdom of Navarre. Thofe extraordinary and fudden reverfes of fortune which mark this whole reign, were equally vifible here. Pampelona was taken, and the whole furrounding country reduced to fubjection; but the rafhnefs and imprudence of the French commander foon reftored to Spain all fhe had loft, and obliged him to evacuate his new conqueft.

Numberlefs fources of difcord fomented the natural rivalfhip of the two monarchs; and Charles, more cautious, and carrying his views farther into futurity than the king of France, had already entered into a ftrict alliance with Leo the tenth, and

fixed

fixed the wavering pontiff in his interests. The re-establishment of Francisco Sforza, Maximilian's brother, in the duchy of Milan, was the grand connecting tie of this confederacy. So visibly replete with future woes did it appear, that Chievres, the emperor's governor and preceptor, when he received the news, expired of sorrow, in the sad anticipation of the calamities which must result from it; often repeating, "Ah! how many evils!"—His prediction was but too exactly verified.

A singular accident befel Francis at this time.—He was at Romorantin in Berri during the winter: according to the manners of the age, when an exertion of vigour or activity characterised and constituted almost every diversion, the king, with a small band of nobles attacked the count de St. Pol's house, who defended it with another party. Snow-balls were used by the assailants: the seigneur de Lorges, one of the opposite side, unfortunately threw down a torch of wood, which struck the king upon the head, and wounded him feverely. He was long confined by this blow; and as it became neceſſary to cut off his hair, he never would ſuffer it to grow again, but introduced the faſhion of wearing the beard long, and the hair ſhort; which ſubſiſted generally in Europe till the reign of Louis the thirteenth, when the ancient cuſtom was reſumed.

The war which had long menaced, at length began. Both princes, concealing in ſome degree their animoſity, and preſerving the laſt appearances, only abetted and ſupported their reſpective vaſſals. The deſire, common to each, of gaining the king of England, who profeſſed himſelf the arbiter of their diſputes, obliged to a certain moderation and delicacy: but this veil was ſoon withdrawn; and Francis, at the head of a gallant army, impatient to ſignalize his valour, and renew the laurels won at Marignano, faced his antagoniſt on the banks of the Schelde.—Here began the fatal train of errors, which in the event reduced France

to

to the moſt calamitous condition. The command of the van belonged to Charles of Bourbon, in right of his office as conſtable: but the king, who never loved him, and whom the reſentment of his mother had ſtill farther prepoſſeſſed in his disfavour, choſe to confide this important truſt to the duke of Alençon, firſt prince of the blood. Not ſatisfied with this cruel and unjuſt affront, he added to it another not leſs injurious to his own fame. The emperor, deſirous of avoiding an engagement, and fearful that from the vicinity of their forces, he might be unavoidably compelled to it, diſlodged with ſome confuſion, and retired under cover of a thick fog to a greater diſtance. Bourbon ſaw the opportunity, and implored his ſovereign to profit of it; but Francis, jealous of a participation which muſt deprive him of part of the honour, and preferring the gratification of his own pique to more glorious and ſalutary principles, rejected with a cold contempt the conſtable's advice; and refuſed to seize the occasion, which never returned, of combating his rival in person.

These repeated insults sunk deep into Bourbon's mind, though as yet they produced no apparent effect. Stung however with the preference given to the duke of Alençon, so contrary to equity or reason; he could not prevent himself from saying, conscious of the quarter from whence he was attacked, " That the king had fol-
" lowed the impressions of a woman, who
" had no more regard to justice, than she
" had honour."—The great lines of his character, which form a contrast to those of Francis, contributed to encrease their mutual dislike. Of a steady courage, attempered, and ever master of itself, he was calculated to command, and capable of the most arduous military atchievements. No general of his age possessed in so extended a degree, the capacity of conciliating the affections of the soldiery, and moulding them to all his purposes. Magnanimous, and liberal where prudence required it, he was naturally œconomical,

nomical. Silent, reflective, and inclined to taciturnity, he did not cultivate the arts of ingratiating himfelf: but wrapped in a haughty virtue, which difdained to ftoop even to the honourable means of acquiring favour or popularity, he refufed to owe any thing except to his own merits *,

Qualities,

* Charles of Bourbon was the fecond fon of Gilbert de Montpenfier, who died at Puzzoli, after an unfuccefsful attempt to preferve the kingdom of Naples, under Charles the eighth. His elder brother, by the moft wonderful and unexampled inftance of filial piety, which hiftory has ever preferved, expired on the tomb of his father, from the pungent and exquifite feelings of diftrefs. His younger brother fell at the battle of Marignano.—The French writers feem generally to infinuate or affert, in terms more or lefs pofitive, that the countefs d'Angoulefme had given him proofs the moft undifguifed, of her attachment; and that the indifference he firft expreffed, and the difdain with which he afterwards treated this paffion, proved the fource of all his future indignities and calamities.

By his marriage with Sufanna of Bourbon, he inherited the immenfe poffeffions of that houfe; his

Qualities, such as those I have depictured, are not framed to raise their possessors in courts, and least of all in that of Francis the first. Bonnivet, who engrossed the royal grace and patronage; and whose ascendancy over his master's mind, produced the most deplorable consequences to France, is an evincing proof of my assertion. He resembled the first Villiers,

own paternal fortunes being limited and slender, Louis the twelfth had chiefly conduced to form this union, by his authority and personal interposition. When the nuptials were solemnized, the young duchess made a solemn and formal contract, by which, in case of her decease, she called to her succession Charles her husband, and endowed him with all her lands, rights, and pretensions. The nature of this donation in presence of the reigning sovereign, and confirmed by his express consent and approval, seemed to secure it from any doubts relative to its validity—but as Susanna, at the time of the request, wanted two or three months to be of age; this unimportant and unnecessary form became eventually the pretext, on which Louisa and the chancellor du Prat founded their infamous and unjust pretensions. She died in childbed about eight years after her marriage, leaving no issue.

duke

KINGS OF FRANCE, &c.

duke of Buckingham, in many points of view. The handsomest cavalier of the court, he was likewise the most arrogant, vain, and presumptuous: born with no talents for war, except courage, he yet had the command of armies entrusted to his care. Gallant and amorous, he was acceptable to women; and peculiarly so to Louisa of Savoy, under whose protection he rose,—Pertinacious in his schemes or determinations, and blinded by his opinion of himself, he never yielded to the advice of others, however disinterested or judicious: yet subservient to the purposes of greatness, and ministering with address to his sovereign's passion for pleasures and dissipation, he acquired, and retained an almost unlimited influence over him.—Being sent into Navarre at the head of a considerable body of forces, he besieged and took Fontarabia. True policy would have dictated the demolition of the fortifications; but Bonnivet proud of his conquest, and desirous of perpetuating its renown, would not hearken to the duke

of

of Guife's remonftrances on that head. The place was garrifoned, and foon after retaken by the Spaniards.

But in Italy, where the emperor and Leo had openly declared hoftilities, the grand operations of war drew Francis's chief attention. He had committed the government of the Milanefe to Odet de Foix, vifcount of Lautrec, and brother to his celebrated miftrefs, madame de Chateau-Briant *. This nobleman, to whom fo important a charge was confided, had fcarce any thing to juftify the choice, except his fifter's favour. He furpaffed even Bonnivet in haughtinefs, and had already

* We know very little with certainty relative to this lady, or the manner of her firft becoming connected with the king. Her name was Françoife de Foix. She was married to the feigneur de Laval in Bretagne. Her influence appears to have lafted till the king's campaign into Italy, which was followed by the battle of Pavia. Mademoifelle de Heilly fucceeded to her place on Francis's return. Her death has been the fubject of much inquiry and romance. It is pretended, probably without reafon, that her veins were opened, by her hufband's command.

difgufted

disgusted the great feudatory lords of the duchy, by his insupportable demeanour.

At the time when the papal and imperial armies entered the Milanese, Lautrec was in France, having left his brother Lescun to supply his place. The king, anxious for the preservation of his Italian dominions, would have instantly sent him thither; but he, conscious of the disorder which Francis's profusion, and his mother's unsatisfied rapacity, had introduced into the finances, absolutely refused to go, till the necessary sums for the payment of his troops were provided: nor was it before he had received the most solemn and reiterated assurances from Louisa, and those who superintended the public treasures, that the money should follow him, that he began his journey. On his arrival, the enemy retired before him in confusion; but by a neglect of those advantages which their situation and mutinous spirit, ready to revolt, repeatedly offerred him, he was reduced in turn to retreat, after having lost the city and castle

of

of Milan, befides Parma, Placenzia, and feveral inferior places. The joy which Leo the tenth felt at this profperous intelligence, produced an agitation of fpirits fo violent, that it was followed by a fever, of which he died the fifth day.

This event, fo unexpected, and fo injurious to the emperor's affairs, ought to have reftored thofe of Francis: but the very evil which Lautrec had dreaded, and even in fome degree predicted, ruined thefe flattering appearances. The countefs d'Angoulefme, by a procedure the moft pernicious to her fon, the moft derogatory to her own honour, and the interefts of the ftate, had diverted the funds deftined to maintain the troops in Italy, to her own ufe. The precife motive which induced her to this violation of the promifes fhe had made, is fomewhat ambiguous and doubtful. Hatred to the countefs de Chateau-Briant and her brother, is the moft probable, and commonly affigned. The money, amounting to three hundred thoufand ecus, had been depofited with
                                         Semblençai;

Semblençai; but Madame d'Angoulefme demanded them with fuch earneftnefs, and threatened the fuperintendant with fo fevere a vengeance in cafe of refufal, that, overcome by the menaces fhe ufed, and repofing on her affurances of protection in cafe of the king's difpleafure, he yielded. The total lofs of the Milanefe was the refult of this iniquitous and inexcufable abufe of her authority. Lautrec, unaffifted with the fums which had been promifed him, could fcarcely maintain himfelf in the duchy: whilft Francifco Sforza, received into Milan, and fupported by Colonna and his fubjects, ftrengthened himfelf in his new acquifitions.—Lefcun, whom his brother had difpatched into France with the account of his diftrefs, arrived at length, but arrived too late. That favourable occafion, which prefents itfelf in the affairs of war, was paft.

Repeated and unfuccefsful efforts deftroyed the army of Lautrec. After having been compelled by the feditious murmurs of his Swifs auxiliaries, to give battle

battle where a defeat was inevitable, and having vainly befieged Parvia, he funk beneath the torrent of adverfe fortune. Every refource being exhaufted, and winter haftening on, he quitted his government, and returned into France, only attended by two domeftics. Lefcun was immediately invefted in Cremona, and neceffitated to capitulate: all the other places received the imperialifts, and even Genoa revolting, expelled the French.

When Lautrec arrived at court, Francis refufed to admit him to his prefence, or hear his juftification: but having, by means of the conftable, obtained the occafion of fpeaking to his majefty, he accufed the fuperintendants of the finances, with having occafioned all the difafters of the campaign, by withholding the fupplies. Semblençai, terrified, and incapable of other defence, threw the blame upon the king's mother: but Louifa, adding the bafeft inhumanity to her other faults, found means to exculpate herfelf, and to perfuade her fon, that only Semblençai

blençai was criminal. Judges were appointed to examine into this dark affair. The chancellor du Prat was among the number. This man, without integrity, fwayed by no principle of juftice or honour, was devoted to the countefs's interefts or paffions, and procured Semblençai's condemnation. The good old man, who had grown grey under four princes, and whom Francis ufed to honour with the endearing and refpectful appellation of his father, was led out to punifhment and ignominioufly executed.—Lautrec, difgraced, was ordered to his government of Guenne *.

Notwith-

* The moft candid and impartial furvey muft acquit Lautrec of blame, or any imputation refpecting the lofs of the Milaneze. He remained with his troops till they became fo mutinous and difcontented, that he was in imminent danger of being feized by them, as a pledge for the payment of their arrears; and was obliged to pafs difguifed through Switzerland, in his return to France. The conftable of Bourbon, not without great difficulty, procured him at length an audience of the king in council, by declaring to

his

Notwithſtanding his paſt misfortunes, and in defiance of almoſt all the great powers

his majeſty, that he could fully juſtify himſelf; and would unfold ſome extraordinary ſecrets, with which it imported him deeply to be made acquainted.

Lautrec, when introduced into the royal preſence, preſerved undiminiſhed his native haughtineſs of deportment; and even preſumed to complain highly to his maſter, of the ungracious reception he gave him. Francis was covered with aſtoniſhment at the recital made him. He ordered Semblençai to be inſtantly ſent for; but in the interval which elapſed between this order and his appearance, he yet reproached Lautrec with incapacity and precipitancy in abandoning the Milaneze, notwithſtanding the diſappointment in his remittances; and added inſultingly, that Colonna and Peſcara, the imperial commanders, had been no better ſupplied, or punctually ſuccoured. To theſe charges Lautrec modeſtly replied; and was engaged in his exculpation, when Semblençai arrived. The king regarded him with a look of furious indignation at his entrance, and demanded if the facts alledged againſt him were true. On the accuſal of his mother as the origin of all theſe evils, his amazement and fury were heightened.—Louiſa was ſummoned, and appeared. Semblençai repeated before her his juſtification.—The counteſs, unawed either by her own conſciouſneſs of its veracity,

powers of Europe combined againſt him, the king perſiſted in his reſolution to recover the Milaneſe. He ſent his favourite Bonnivet, lately created admiral, over the mountains, and had intended to command the army in perſon deſtined to this enterprize; when a conſpiracy the moſt alarming and important checked his deſigns, and compelled him to watch over the tranquillity of his kingdom. I mean the conſtable's defection and revolt.

If ever treaſon was palliated by the circumſtances which attended or produced it—if a crime ſo ſtigmatized and degrading, admits of apology or defence, it muſt be in the perſon of Charles of Bourbon. This nobleman, whom his birth, his qualities, his power and offices under

city, or by the preſence of the king, gave a looſe to the moſt unbounded reſentment againſt the unfortunate treaſurer, and ſcrupled not to accuſe him of a lie, and to demand vengeance as of a traitor, who had aſperſed her honour.—Semblençai's ruin and execution were the conſequence of this iniquitous and foul tranſaction.

the crown, ought to have raised above the persecution of any individual, had been marked out by the countess d'Angoulesme's unrelenting and incessant desire of vengeance. It is said, that the contempt with which he had refused her hand and person, which she offered him, superadded to the unconcealed sentiments of detestation which he avowed for her character, had inflamed her to a pitch of resentment, which could only be satiated by his ruin. Bonnivet, thirsting for the sword of constable, and hoping to obtain it by his disgrace, joined the countess; and du Prat, the most corrupt and vicious minister to whom the seals were ever confided, lent his aid to complete the scheme.

Not content to have prevented his marriage with the princess Renée, youngest daughter to Louis the twelfth, and sister of the queen; Louisa determined to strike at the root of his greatness, by laying claim to the vast possessions which he had inherited in right of his wife Susanna of Bourbon, daughter to the famous lady of Beaujeau,

Beaujeu, regent under Charles the eighth. She fucceeded, though in contradiction to apparent equity, and by a perverfion of every facred or binding inftitution. The unhappy conftable, oppreffed by unmerited feverity, and driven to defpair by a feries of unparalleled infults, facrificed his loyalty to his defire of revenge; and entered into a treaty with the emperor. Charles, who knew his value, and the important confequences which might enfue from fuch a chieftain gained, accorded, and exceeded all his demands *.

Francis

---

* Adrian de Croy, count de Rieux, and firft gentleman of the bedchamber, was the perfon employed by the emperor to carry on the negotiation with Bourbon. He paffed through France difguifed as a peafant, and arrived by night at Chantelle, the conftable's feat in Auvergne, where he lay in an adjoining apartment to him, and fettled the terms previous to his revolt. Charles, not fatisfied with the powers granted to the count de Rieux, and defirous of entering into more exact conditions with the emperor, difpatched La Mothe de Noyers, a gentleman in his fervice, into Spain. He returned, bring-

Francis received advice of this dangerous confpiracy as he was on his rout to Lyons, in the intent of croffing the Alps; and he inftantly took the refolution of coming to an explanation with the conftable in perfon. He went to him at Moulins, and informed him candidly of the imputation laid to his charge. Bourbon

ing with him the moft ample and general ratification of his demands. Bourbon buried the papers in a box under ground, at the foot of a tree; and began to affemble his partizans and vaffals, in the pretence of accompanying the king into Italy. Matignon and d'Argouges, two gentlemen of that number, and who were privy to their lord's confpiracy, having confeffed at Eafter to a prieft, and enumerated, among their other tranfgreffions, a plot againft the ftate in which they were engaged; he commanded them inftantly to avow it to their fovereign, and fet out immediately himfelf to impart this interefting intelligence to Brezé, fenechal of Normandy. The gentlemen believing themfelves loft, and confcious that their confeffion could alone preferve their lives, mounted on horfeback; and meeting Francis at St. Pierre-le-Moutier in the Bourbonnois, threw themfelves at his feet, and made an ingenuous difclofure of the whole tranfaction.

denied his having accepted the emperor's offers, though he confeſſed overtures had been made to ſhake his allegiance. As this confeſſion was ſufficient to juſtify his ſeizure, it was either owing to the king's generoſity, and conſciouſneſs how unworthily he had been treated; or to his incapacity of arreſting ſo powerful a lord, environed by vaſſals who adored him; that he was not committed to cuſtody. Francis only commanded him to follow him to Lyons. Bourbon affected to obey; and being ſomewhat indiſpoſed, began his journey in a litter. While he was on the way, intelligence was brought him that the parliament, in purſuance of the ſentence paſſed againſt him, had ordered all his lands to be ſequeſtered. Wounded anew by this information, he yet attempted to ward the blow; and hoping from Francis's generous magnanimity what Louiſa refuſed, he diſpatched the biſhop of Autun, to implore that this decree might at leaſt be ſuſpended; and aſſuring the king that ſuch an act of grace and tenderneſs would

would bind him for ever to his service. Had his request been granted, there is the highest reason to suppose, it would have retained him in his duty; but by the inveterate animosity of his enemies, who had resolved his destruction, the bishop was arrested at only two leagues distance*.

Losing

---

* The minutest circumstances respecting the flight of so great a man become interesting.—When the bishop of Autun was seized by the marechal de Chabannes, a footman galloped in all haste to give the constable information of it. He was then at Chantelle. The instant he received this news, he set out by night for Herman, a town of Auvergne, where Henry Arnauld, a gentleman attached to him, was governor. He arrived during the darkness, and awoke Pomperant and Montagnac-Tenzane immediately.—The former of these owed his life to him; for having killed Chisay, a celebrated gallant of the court, Bourbon sheltered him, and afterwards procured his pardon.—Tenzane, aged near eighty years at this time, remained inviolably attached to him in his misfortunes, though he had ever opposed and been averse to his treaty with the emperor. It was requisite that one should accompany him, while the other favoured his flight. As the latter employment was by far the most hazardous, it became a subject of contest, both

desiring

Losing all expectation of soothing Francis's anger, after so manifest a declaration of it, he returned to his castle of Chantelle; and hearing that four thousand men were on their march to invest him in it, he quitted it by night with torches. After having walked some way, he contrived to deceive his attendants, and withdrew from them unobserved. They, attached to their lord in his misfortunes, would not abandon him; and continued to follow Francis de Montagnac-Tenzane, who had taken his horse and habit, in the apprehension that it was the constable. Daybreak shewed them their mistake; and Tenzane, addressing them with tears, informed them, that their master had taken another road; that he thanked them for

desiring ardently this desperate commission. Chance alone decided it in favour of Tenzane. He executed it with the most consummate address, and afterwards rejoined his master in Italy.—The constable and Pomperant crossed all the county of Burgundy, having only made use of one precaution, that of shoeing their horses backwards.

their

their unshaken fidelity and affection; and besought them to repair to their own houses till farther order. — Meanwhile Bourbon continued his flight. Only one gentleman accompanied him, named Pomperant. He soon gained the Franche Comté, and from thence passing through Trent to Mantua, arrived safe at Genoa. No revolt or rebellion succeeded; nor did the king make any minute researches into the accomplices or abettors of the constable's intrigues. Shame and generosity pleading in his bosom for his injured subject, probably prevented him.

Amid these convulsions of the state, died Claude queen of France. Historians, lost among the crowd of battles and public transactions which diversify this reign, have scarce deigned to mark her death. She was called, "The good Queen," from her many amiable qualities and virtues; but her person corresponded not to the beauty of her mind. She was somewhat lame like her mother, Anne of Bretagne; and in other respects little calculated to retain

retain the affections of a hufband, gallant, inconftant, and fond of pleafure. She neither interfered in affairs of policy, or poffeffed any afcendancy over the king. Madame d'Angoulefme retained the whole authority. Her end was accelerated, if not abfolutely produced, by a difeafe which Francis communicated to her, and which was the refult of his irregular and promifcuous intercourfe with women. She expired at the caftle of Blois, only twenty-four years old, and after having borne feven children [*].

Though the dread of fome inteftine commotion prevented the king from en-

---

[*] Anne of Bretagne predicted her daughter's fortune, if married to the count d'Angoulefme; but Louis the twelfth, with that goodnefs fo uniformly vifible in his character, replied to her remonftrances, "Vous " vous trompez; elle n'eft pas belle, mais fa vertu " touchera le Comte, et il ne pourra s'empecher de lui " rendre juftice."—Francis hardly juftified this favourable opinion of him. Brantome does not fcruple to fay, in terms the moft exprefs, that he gave her a venereal diftemper of the worft kind, which terminated in her death.

tering

tering Italy in perſon at this time, yet Bonnivet continued his march, and reached the Milaneſe, unoppoſed. Had he purſued the advantages which his unexpected appearance, and the diſorder among the imperial troops, afforded him, the whole duchy might have been regained to France: but he neglected them, till the approach of winter, and the plague, which made a rapid progreſs among his ſoldiery, neceſſitated him to retire. Bourbon, to whom Charles had confided the ſupreme command of his armies, in conjunction with Lannoy, viceroy of Naples, and the marquis of Peſcara, followed the admiral with that impetuous and eager haſte, which the wiſh of vengeance on his declared and mortal enemy lent him. Bonnivet, wounded in the arm, and dreading more than death to fall into the conſtable's hands, left Bayard, ſo renowned in the annals of chivalry, to cover the retreat of his forces; and putting himſelf into a litter, arrived ſafe at Lyons. Bayard executed the charge committed to him with that noble intrepidity

pidity which has immortalized his name, but fell in the execution of it; and after his death, the French having totally evacuated Italy, every place in the Milanese returned to the emperor.

These succeſſes emboldened Bourbon to enter Provence. His own intentions were to have pushed on without delay into the interior provinces of the kingdom, where he expected to have been joined by all his vaſſals; but Charles's generals, attentive only to their maſter's intereſts, compelled him to adopt other counſels, and laid ſiege to Marſeilles. It was gallantly and obſtinately defended; and after a blockade of ſix weeks, the Imperial commanders, alarmed at Francis's approach with a conſiderable army, diſlodged in confuſion; and re-embarking the greater part of their artillery, retreated with expedition acroſs the mountains.

The king, naturally ſanguine, and eaſily elated by the favours of fortune, determined to follow the conſtable by great marches. Bonnivet urged him to this

raſh

rash project, and represented the condition of the Milanese defenceless and unprotected; the precipitate retreat of the Imperialists, dejected and dismayed. Superadded to these public motives, it is said a private one, not inconsistent with Francis's character — his desire to visit a beautiful lady of Milan, whom the admiral had depictured to him in colours the most animated and flattering, still farther induced him to it *. His oldest and wisest generals opposed the strongest reasons to dissuade him. They represented the state of his kingdom left open to the invasions of Charles and Henry; the

* This story is not so improbable, or ill-founded, as at first we may be inclined to suppose. Brantome, who was well acquainted with the intrigues of Francis's court, declares this in the most positive manner, as a secret known to few. He says, that her name was, " La Signora Clerice," a noble lady of Milan, and esteemed one of the finest women in Italy; that Bonnivet had obtained from her the last favours some years before, and inflamed the king with the same desire. The more we consider the characters of the admiral and his prince, the more are we inclined to credit this narration.

near

near approach of winter, and advanced feafon. Louifa, as if from a prefentiment of the calamities which her fon's conduct would entail on France, ufed every method to prevent it. As foon as fhe received notice of his intention to enter Italy, fhe difpatched three fucceffive couriers to ftop his march; or, if that could not be, at leaft to implore him to wait till fhe had embraced, and bid him a laft adieu. The king was deaf to her entreaties or remonftrances; and ordered her to be informed by the laft meffenger, that he was too far advanced to think of fufpending his progrefs, but that he invefted her with the regency during his abfence.

Francis's entry into the Milanefe fpread equal or greater terror, than Bonnivet's and Lautrec's had done in former campaigns. Bourbon, purfued in turn by; his adverfary, and flying before thofe whom he had fo lately driven, fcarce could avoid being overtaken. The French followed fo clofe upon his fteps, that their

troops

troops even entered one of the gates of Milan, only half an hour after he had escaped by another; and had the king perfisted not to allow them time for recovery, from the consternation into which he had thrown them, no exertion of military skill in Charles's commanders could have prevented their defeat, or mutiny and separation. Unhappily, the admiral's advice, and ascendancy over his master, prevented him from embracing this salutary conduct; and prevailed on him, in opposition to the universal voice of his captains, to undertake the siege of Pavia.—The sequel is so well known to all Europe, that it is a needless task to recite it. The fatal day when Francis became the emperor's prisoner, has been related by so many historians, and with such a minute enumeration of the facts which accompanied and followed it, that I shall not enter on the narration. Some circumstances rather relating to the Individual than the Monarch, and which History has considered confidered as beneath its dignity to recount, I fhall mention.

The king gave in that celebrated engagement the moft diftinguifhed proofs of courage and prowefs; nor was it to any want of military virtue, that his misfortunes are to be imputed. The number and the quality of thofe whom he killed with his own hand, are inconteftable evidences of this affertion. His armour rendered him diftinguifhed in the field, by its richnefs and fplendour; whereas Bourbon, more cautious and circumfpect, combated in the habit of a private cavalier, having given Pomperant his troop to lead. Thrown from his horfe, wounded, fpent with fatigue, and almoft deferted by his followers, Francis continued to defend himfelf with a valour the moft obftinate. Two Spanifh gentlemen, Diego d'Avila, and Juan d'Orbieta, put their fwords to his throat. In this exigency, a follower of Bourbon's, named La Mothe de Noyers; came up, and knowing the king, though his face was covered with

blood,

blood, called out to him to furrender to the conftable, who was not far off: but difdaining to deliver up his fword to a man whom he regarded as a traitor, he refufed, and demanded Lannoy. While La Mothe ran every where in hope to difcover his lord, the viceroy of Naples arrived at the fpot, and received Francis's fubmiffions. This was a peculiar good fortune, as Bourbon would certainly have taken him by force from any perfon of inferior authority or diftinction.

Diego d'Avila firft pulled off his gauntlets, and the furrounding crowd defpoiled him of his coat of mail, his belt, and fpurs.—Meanwhile the marquis del Guafto approached the king, and faluted him with great refpect; and, as he requefted with peculiar earneftnefs, that he might not be led into the city of Pavia for a mockery to the inhabitants, the marquis conducted him to his own tent. The wounds he had received in the action were infpected, and carefully dreffed. One was near the eyebrow, another in the arm,

and

and a third in his right hand. Besides these, he had received several balls from a harquebusse in his cuirass. The marquis del Guasto had the honour to sup with him; and Bourbon presented the napkin to his majesty. The Spanish historians declare that he received it very graciously, and even permitted the constable to kiss his hand on the knee; but the French writers assert the contrary, and say he turned his back on him with contempt, and would not take the napkin from him. During his repast, the discourse naturally turned on the past action; and Francis, with infinite modesty, propriety, and eloquence, pointed out the causes which conduced to its loss, and chiefly blamed the cowardice of the Switzers and Italians in his army. When he retired to rest, none of his valets being near to aid him to undress, a certain sieur de Montpezat, who had been made prisoner by a Spanish soldier, presented himself for that purpose; and the king, pleased with his humble assiduity and attention, redeemed, and elevated

elevated him to the dignity of a marechal of France.

Many renowned commanders perifhed on that day: Lefcun and Bonnivet were among the chief. The latter expiated, in fome meafure, his fatal advice, by the gallantry and courage with which he devoted himfelf to death. Seeing the fortune of the battle waver, and the troops difpofed to fly, he attempted to rally the Switzers, and fome cavalry: but not being able to fucceed, and no hope remaining of victory, he raifed the vizor of his helmet, that he might be univerfally known; and rufhing into the thickeft ranks of the enemy, oppofed his breaft to their fwords, and fell, covered with honourable wounds. Bourbon had given exprefs orders to take him alive if poflible; and, in cafe that was not poflible, to kill him; in no cafe to let him efcape. After the engagement, his body was found; and the conftable ftanding over it, and having confidered it long in filence, only exclaimed, "Ah! malheureux! Tu es caufe de
" la

"la ruine de la France, et de la mienne!" The duke of Alençon, who had been married to the celebrated Margaret of Valois, fifter of Francis, behaved unworthy his rank as prince of the blood. He fled among the firft, and retired to Lyons with a number of the nobility, where he died in a few days of grief and fhame. The king of Navarre, Henry d'Albret, remained a prifoner.

Lannoy was meanwhile in the utmoft anxiety how to difpofe of his royal captive. The day after the action, he conducted him to the caftle of Pizzhigitone, where he remained two months under the care of Don Fernand Alarçon. No pofitive orders arriving from the emperor's council in Spain, for his removal to another fortrefs, the viceroy of Naples became more apprehenfive of fome accident, which might procure or terminate in his enlargement. The Imperial troops, who had fcarcely received any pay, were difpofed to mutiny, and might eafily feize on his perfon to enfure their arrears.

To carry him to the caftle of Naples, where he might have been fecurely detained, was a much more eligible plan; but they dreaded left the pope or the Venetians might attempt to refcue him on the road. It was ftill more hazardous to transfer him into Spain by fea, becaufe the gallies of Andrea Doria, and of France, were ftationed to intercept his paffage.— Lannoy's addrefs extricated him from thefe numerous difficulties. He found means to engage the king to embrace thofe meafures, of his own accord, which otherwife it would have been impoffible to execute; and perfuaded him that a perfonal interview with Charles, was the fpeedieft method of adjufting fo weighty an affair, and reftoring him to freedom. Francis, who, generous himfelf, fuppofed others to have hearts equally magnanimous and enlarged, eagerly caught at the infidious propofal, and fell into the fnare. To fuch a pitch of punctilious honour did he carry his fentiments, that he even oppofed himfelf to a fedition among the Imperial

Imperial foldiery, of which he might have profited; and not only commanded Doria to make no attempt on the Spanifh veffels which conducted him from Italy, but caufed the regent to lend fix gallies to Lannoy. About the middle of June they fet fail from Portofiero, and arrived happily at Alicant. The king was brought under a ftrong guard to Madrid, and lodged in the caftle *.

The confternation and public affright which Francis's defeat and captivity fpread throughout the whole kingdom, is equalled by nothing in the French annals, except the capture of John at the battle of Poitiers. Louifa, his mother, exclaimed at the fad news, in the recollection of her reiterated, but ineffectual efforts to ftop

* I muft own myfelf more indebted to Brantome, than to any other author, for moft of the particulars I have enumerated, relative to the battle of Pavia. The memoirs of Du Bellay, and thofe of De Thou, contain many curious remarks. " Les anec-
" dotes des reines et regentes de France," together with Mezeray, furnifh likewife matter of entertainment and information.

his march over the mountains, " Helas! " il ne m'a voulu croire; ha! que je lui " avois tant dit!"—Though oppreſſed by every feeling of parental woe; though originally the author of theſe calamities, by her malevolent and unjuſt perſecution of Bourbon; though unpopular, and holding the regency, in this convulſion of the ſtate, by a tenure the moſt precarious; ſhe neverthelefs ſuſtained her courage. She did more, and even effaced, in a great meaſure, her paſt offences, by the wiſdom, vigour, and uniformity of her conduct. Henry the eighth of England, the Venetian republic, and the reigning pontiff, Clement the ſeventh, were all induced to quit the emperor's party by her ſolicitations. She negotiated in every court, and moved all the ſprings which can actuate ſtateſmen or politicians, to effect her ſon's releaſe.

During theſe endeavours of the regent, Francis had time to diſcover and repent the error, into which his romantic generoſity and honour had led him. Inſtead of of the interview with which he had been flattered; inſtead of treating with his conqueror, as from gentleman to gentleman; inſtead of that courteous and noble reception which he had expected, and which every part of his own behaviour intitled him to receive; he found a ſolitary priſon, guards inexorable and vigilant, a confinement unuſually ſevere and ſtrict.— Charles did not deign to ſee him in this rigorous captivity; and the only recreation permitted him, was to take the air on a mule, ſurrounded with ſoldiers. This unworthy and unkingly uſage, continued for ſix months, produced a fever, the effect of diſappointment and vexation. The arrival of the ducheſs of Alençon, his beloved ſiſter, to whom the emperor had granted permiſſion to viſit him in this diſtreſsful ſituation, conduced principally to his recovery : and Charles himſelf, aſhamed of his cruel inſenſibility, and terrified leſt his priſoner's death might rob him of the vaſt advantages he doubted not to derive from his releaſe, conde-

condefcended to make him a fhort, but confolatory vifit; in which he affected the utmoft commiferation, and gave him profpects of fpeedy freedom. Thefe fallacious expectations vanifhed with the king's return of health; and, in the defpair of regaining his liberty, except on conditions fo humiliating and ignominious as to preclude any acceptance of them, he entrufted to his fifter, on her return, a deed, by which he refigned his kingdom to the dauphin Francis, his eldeft fon. Margaret carried this act of refignation into France.

Charles, touched at length, not by motives of generofity or greatnefs of foul, but by apprehenfions of intereft and narrow policy;—viewing the ftate of the Milanefe, left defencelefs by the marquis de Pefcara's death, and a great league formed for the releafe of Francis—entered into a treaty with him. Even then he did not relax the rigor of his demands; though Gattinara, his chancellor, predicted their certain violation, and refufed, with un-
fubmitting

KINGS OF FRANCE, &c. 233

submitting firmness, to affix to them the seals. — The marriage of the emperor's sister, Eleanor of Portugal, with the king, formed the cement of this famous treaty: but the restitution of Burgundy was an article so injurious to the state, so ruinous and fatal in its nature, that the king protested against it in private, previous to his departure from Madrid.

After a captivity of near thirteen months from the battle of Pavia, he was reconducted by his two keepers, Lannoy and Alarçon, to the bank of the river Bidassoa, near Fontarabia: while Lautrec brought the two young sons of France, the dauphin and his brother Henry, who were to be delivered up as hostages for their father, to the opposite side. The exchange was made, and Francis once more entered his kingdom.—At Bayonne he found Louisa and Margaret, who attended his arrival. The interview between them was touching and lively, in the highest degree. The countess d'Angoulesme, who knew the constitution of her son, and his disposition

position to gallantry, had prepared for him fetters of a softer nature than those he had experienced at Madrid. She prefented to him the celebrated Mademoifelle de Heilly, better known under the title of duchefs of Eftampes. Her age at this time did not exceed eighteen years. A beauty of perfon the moft delicate and perfect, fuperadded to wit, and an underftanding improved by all the cultivation of the age, enfured her conqueft over the king. He became paffionately attached to her; and their connection lafted in its full force during the remainder of his life.

Here let us paufe a moment! The re-entry of Francis into his dominions forms a new epocha in his reign.

CHAPTER

CHAPTER THE SEVENTH.

Treaty of Madrid violated.—War renewed between Francis and the Emperor.—Unsuccessful attack of Naples.—Death of Lautrec.—Peace of Cambray.—Marriage of Francis to Eleanor of Portugal.—Magnificence of the king.—Death of his mother, Louisa.—Interview of Marseilles.—Marriage of the duke of Orleans to Catherine of Medicis.—War renewed.—The Emperor enters Provence.—Death of Francis, the Dauphin.—Circumstances of it.—His character.—Reflections.—The Emperor retreats into Italy.—Marriage of James the fifth to the princess Magdalen.—Character of Anne de Montmorenci.—Interviews of Nice and Aigues-Mortes.—Story of the cave in Dauphiné.—Francis's amours.—Indisposition, and consequent change.—Visit of the Emperor.—Alteration of the ministers.—Third war.—Description of the court.—Battle of Cerizoles.—The

Emperor enters Picardy.—Intrigues of the duchefs of Eftampes.—Peace concluded.— Death of the duke of Orleans.—Circumſtances.—Character.—Death of the Count d'Enguien.—Parties formed in the court. —Francis's illneſs.—Circumſtances.—Dying admonitions to the dauphin.—Death.— Character.

FRANCIS the firſt was ſtill in the prime of life when his impriſonment terminated, and he ſaw himſelf again reſtored to his throne and people. His misfortunes, and conſequent captivity, though they had not made ſo deep an impreſſion on him, as to alter eſſentially his character, yet rendered him more circumſpect and cautious in his conduct. The raſh and impetuous valour which had diſtinguiſhed him hitherto, was calmed, and attempered into a ſerener courage: and policy, or intereſts of ſtate, compelled him to adopt meaſures leſs diſintereſted, and better adapted to the temper of the emperor,

his

his antagonift.—But thefe were only partial changes: his magnificence, ever accompanied with profufion; his unreftrained attachment and liberality to favourites; his paffion for women, and all the luxurious diffipations of a court; thefe errors yet characterifed him in the moft extended degree: and, by introducing confufion into his finances, and a diforder through every department of government, gave Charles a fuperiority in the affairs of war, and involved his kingdom in numberlefs evils.

So oppreffive and fevere were the conditions of the treaty of Madrid, that the king, confcious his infringement of them would be approved and defended through all Europe, no fooner recovered his freedom, than he declared to Lannoy, who had accompanied him to demand their execution; that Burgundy, being a part, not of the royal domain, but of the kingdom, could not be alienated or difmembered by any exertion of the regal authority. He difpenfed himfelf from his oaths,

oaths, as compulsory, and the effect of neceffity; and, having tendered other ceffions and offers for the releafe of his children, and for a final peace, prepared himfelf to exert new military efforts to compel the emperor to the acceptance of them. In this defign, a great league was concluded at the caftle of Cognac in Angoumois, whither he had retired, during the fummer, to enjoy the pleafures of the chace. The powers confederated were, Francis, the pope, Sforza, the Venetians, and Florentines.

Had their combined forces attacked the Milanefe, deftitute either of troops or commanders, without delay, it muft have been inevitably re-conquered: but a negligence and inattention to thefe manifeft advantages, equally extraordinary and blameable, gave Bourbon time to arrive, and Lannoy to provide for the fafety of Naples. The former, to whom Charles had promifed the inveftiture of the duchy; after having forced Sforza to furrender the caftle

of

of Milan, and having exhaufted every art
to fatisfy the murmurs of his foldiery, difcontented from the want of pay, took the
daring and defperate refolution of marching to Rome.' He executed it; and, though
killed on the attack by a mufket-fhot under the walls, his victorious army entered,
and pillaged that celebrated city. Clement, who had retired to the caftle of St.
Angelo, was neceffitated to capitulate from
famine, and remained a prifoner in the
emperor's hands.

An outrage fo violent, and even deemed
facrilegious, as that of Charles on the common father of Chriftendom, produced a
new league between Henry the eighth and
Francis. Jealoufy and terror cemented
this alliance. Lautrec, who had long lan-
guifhed under the difpleafure of his prince,
was recalled, and placed at the head of the
army deftined againft Italy. Grown diftruftful by his paft misfortunes, and fore-
feeing, in the character of the king, frefh
fources of future difafter and defeat, he
would

would have declined the honour tendered him: but being obliged to submit to the royal mandate, he prepared to pass the mountains.

The two kings sent their heralds to defy the emperor; who returned these insults by reproaches and invectives against Francis, whom he branded with epithets the most opprobrious, and challenged to single combat. In the impotence of his resentment, he even violated the sacred duties of humanity and clemency, by revenging in some degree the errors of the father on his blameless children. He not only rendered the confinement of the young dauphin and the duke of Orleans unusually strict; but shut them up in apartments darkened, and did not permit them any sort of diversion or amusement. His visits and notice of them were short, cold, and unfrequent; and, by a barbarity unworthy his character, he deprived them of their most faithful and beloved domestics, whom he sent, to work chained in his gallies.

Meanwhile Lautrec again entered the Milanese, so often conquered, and so often lost. With the fortune constantly attendant on the French arms at their first arrival, he rapidly reduced it to subjection. On the news of his approach, the Imperial generals released the sovereign pontiff, and hastily evacuated Rome. Lautrec pursued them by great marches; and, presenting battle to their troops, enervated by plunder, and thinned by pestilential diseases, the effects of their intemperance and licentiousness, drove them before him in confusion. Naples afforded them an asylum. It is said, that had he improved their panic, and laid instant siege to the place, he might have hoped every thing from their general disorder and dismay: but he lost that favourable juncture, in the attack of several inferior towns, and at length sat down before it.

By that unhappy fatality which seemed to accompany the enterprizes of Francis beyond the Alps, but which was really the necessary

neceſſary conſequence of his own negligent remiſſneſs, and deſultory reſolutions, or unequal meaſures, all theſe promiſing appearances were overclouded, and rendered finally abortive. Lautrec, anxious for his own and his ſovereign's glory; and though defective as a commander, animated with the warmeſt enthuſiaſm for his country, exerted all his endeavours to avert the deſtruction which he had early predicted.—He implored the king to ſatisfy, and conciliate the celebrated Doria, whoſe concurrence and aid to block up the port of Naples, was indiſpenſably requiſite to the capture of the city. It was debated in the cabinet council to comply with this advice: but Du Prat and Montmorenci having ſtrongly oppoſed it, from ſome little motives of private intereſt and emolument, this wholeſome and ſalutary counſel was rejected. The ſiege was unavoidably protracted; ſummer advanced, and diſtempers began to ſpread themſelves among the French: the hopes of ſucceſs grew

grew fainter every day, and the army, almoſt rendered incapable of action by its loſſes, ſunk into univerſal dejection. Lautrec long ſuſtained his courage unſhaken; but ſeized at length with a mortal diſeaſe, he became unable to perform the functions of a general. His officers endeavoured to induce him to retire to Capua: but he had ſworn to enter Naples victorious, or die; and, ſinking under the preſſure rather of intellectual difquietude and pain, than bodily infirmity, he expired in the camp. With him the poor remains of vigour and firmneſs, which yet animated his troops, became extinct. The marquis de Saluzzo, on whom the ſupreme command devolved, capitulated ſoon after, and died in impriſonment. All Naples was evacuated by the French; and theſe vaſt preparations, like ſo many which had preceded them, produced no advantage to the kingdom.

Tired with war, and exhauſted by ſuch continual efforts, the various princes of

Europe suspended, from common weakness, their mutual hostilities. This voluntary truce was followed by a final pacification. Margaret of Burgundy *, aunt to the emperor, and Louisa, mother of Francis, were the mediators of an accommodation so desirable. It was concluded at Cambray; and the terms, though burthensome and severe to France, were yet submitted to, in the passionate wish to rescue the dauphin and his brother

---

* She was a princess of infinite wit and capacity. Her affiance to Charles the eighth having been dissolved from political motives, Margaret was sent back into the Low Countries. She was afterwards demanded by Ferdinand and Isabella, for their only son Don Juan. On her voyage from Flanders into Spain, a violent storm attacked them near the coast of England. The vessel was expected to sink. Amid such a scene of terror and confusion, she had the calmness and presence of mind, to tie all her jewels round her arm in a waxed cloth; annexing these two humorous lines of poetry, descriptive of her peculiar fortune,

" Cy git Margot, la gente Demoiselle,
" Qu'eut deux Maris, et si mourut Pucelle."

from

from their captivity, which formed one of the moſt important articles.

The marechal de Montmorenci was ſent to Andaye, on the frontier of Spain, with the ranſom : while Velaſco, conſtable of Caſtile, conducted the two princes, and Eleanor, the ſiſter of Charles, to the oppoſite ſide of the river. The exchange being reciprocally made, they proceeded towards Bourdeaux. Francis advanced to meet them as far as the abby of Veien in Gaſcony, and the nuptial ceremonies were performed there the ſame day. Eleanor was at this time thirty years of age : her perſon had very few charms ; and the king, already enſlaved to his miſtreſs, the duchefs of Eſtampes, never regarded her with affection, and conſidered the union as merely political. She received, notwithſtanding, all the external honours of royalty, and was ever treated by her huſband with great reſpect. As Montmorenci began likewiſe about this time to acquire a

prodigious

prodigious intereſt and aſcendant over his maſter; the queen, conſcious of her little intrinſic conſequence, attached him to her, and ſupported herſelf by his influence and credit.

During the interval of tranquillity and repoſe which ſucceeded to the almoſt continual wars ſince Francis's acceſſion, he mixed the patronage of letters, and munificent protection of all the liberal arts, with the ſplendour and luxury which eminently diſtinguiſhed his court. The ſimplicity of Louis the twelfth's manners was forgotten; and the introduction of ladies conſtantly about the perſon of the ſovereign, a cuſtom unknown before in Europe, breathed a ſpirit of gallantry, which the king's character and converſation were calculated to encourage. "Une cour "ſans dames," ſaid he frequently, " eſt " une année ſans printemps; une prin- " temps ſans roſes." His ſiſter Margaret,

garet, afterwards queen of Navarre, was one of the moſt accompliſhed princeſſes of whom we read in ſtory. Though the martial ſpirit of chivalry ſtill gave an air of rudeneſs and ferocity to the diverſions and entertainments exhibited; yet an elegance and refinement infenſibly mixed itſelf with them, and began to take off the edge of this remaining barbariſm. Fontainbleau, Chambord, and St. Germain-en-Laye ſucceſſively appeared: and genius, waking at the encouragement extended to it by ſo great a monarch, exerted its firſt attempts in eulogiums to his honour.

The death of the ducheſs of Angouleſme followed ſoon after the peace, which her endeavours had contributed chiefly to produce. Paris being ravaged by the plague, ſhe retired to Fontainbleau; but the environs being infected, obliged her to take the rout of Romorantin in Berri. Sickneſs compelled her to ſtop at Grez, a little village in the Gatinois; and ſhe expired

pired there after a few days illnefs, at fifty-four years of age *.

Though

* Brantome relates a circumſtance of her death, ſtrongly indicative of the ſuperſtitious terrors, to which even princes were not ſuperior, in the ſixteenth century, nor was genius, however elevated, exempt from them.

Three days before ſhe expired, ſays he, being awake during the night, ſhe was ſurprized at an extraordinary brightneſs, which illuminated the chamber. Apprehending it to be the fire which her women made, ſhe reprimanded them; but they replied, that it was cauſed by the moon. The duchefs ordered her curtains to be undrawn; and diſcovered that a comet produced this unuſual light. "Ah!" exclaimed ſhe, " this is a phænomenon that appears not for perſons " of common condition! Shut the window; it is a " comet, which announces my departure: I muſt " prepare myſelf for it."—The enſuing morning ſhe ſent for her confeſſor, in the certainty of her approaching diſſolution. The phyſicians aſſured her, that her apprehenſions were ill-founded and premature. "If I had not ſeen," replied Louiſa, " the ſig- " nal for my death, I could believe it; for I do not " feel myſelf exhauſted or ſpent." She expired on the third day from this event.

It is ſaid ſhe had always extremely dreaded the termination of life, and could never ſupport the mention

Though her masterly and unwearied efforts to procure the king's release, seem in some measure to efface the criminal conduct which preceded it; yet cannot it obliterate the stain of Bourbon's exile, and Semblançai's execution. She was more lamented by her son, than by his people; and seems to have been quickly forgotten by both. Francis solemnized her funerals with his accustomed magnificence, and interred her at St. Denis, among the sovereigns of France; and Adulation, ever ready to celebrate even the imaginary virtues of the great, crowned her tomb with laurels and panegyrics.

The alliance between France and England still subsisted. The two kings, mutually desirous of cementing it, met at St.

---

tion of mortality, even from the pulpit. Long after this period, and even late in the last century, all the appearances of the celestial bodies, not perfectly comprehended by the multitude, were supposed to indicate and foretel the deaths of sovereigns, or changes and revolutions of empires.

Joquelvert,

Joquelvert, a little village between Calais and Boulogne. Every mark of mutual confidence, honour, and friendſhip, was ſhewn by each in turn, and all the appearances of a perfect union diſplayed in their behaviour. We find no period of hiſtory, when the interviews of monarchs were ſo common and frequent as in the ſixteenth century, and more peculiarly under this reign; yet none, where the compacts entered into were ſo ſoon violated, and the wars ſo obſtinate, and continually renewed.

This conference was followed, in the enſuing year, by another of higher conſequence, and greater ſplendor: I mean the famous interview of Marſeilles. Francis, intoxicated with the wiſh to reconquer the Milaneſe, adapted all his meaſures to that great purpoſe. He courted all the Italian princes, and eſpecially the houſe of Medicis, as capable of being made eminently ſubſervient to his views on the duchy. Theſe motives determined him to enter

into

into the clofeft connections with Clement, the reigning pope, by demanding Catherine, his niece, in marriage for Henry duke of Orleans. The pontiff, flattered by this condefcenfion in fo great a monarch, and paffionately anxious to aggrandife his family, accepted the offer with a pleafure he did not affect to conceal. The king's gallies conducted him and the princefs into France. Francis, attended by the queen and his whole court, made his entry into Marfeilles the day following that of his holinefs. The nuptials were celebrated with uncommon magnificence, and the feftivities continued during five weeks. Henry and Catherine were both in very early youth. Their ages only differed by thirteen days, nor had either of them completed their fourteenth year: yet Clement, fearful left from the change of political circumftances, the marriage, if not completed, might be liable to a diffolution, demanded its inftant confummation; which was performed the fame night. The king
founded

founded vast expectations on this alliance, in case of future hostilities with the emperor; but the untimely death of the pope, which happened only eleven months afterwards, dissipated, and rendered them ineffectual.

New causes of discontent between these powerful and inveterate rivals increased continually, and portended the renewal of those convulsions which had already interested and disturbed all Europe. Francis first openly appeared in arms. The execution of his agent at Milan, whom Francisco Sforza, in the intention of gratifying Charles, had caused to be privately put to death in prison, formed a pretext for the rupture: and as the duke of Savoy had likewise given many causes of umbrage and dissatisfaction, besides the refusal of permission to his troops to pass through Piedmont, he no longer preserved any measures with that prince. Brion, lately created admiral, entered, and subjected, almost without a blow, his whole dominions;

dominions; while he vainly implored the emperor's protection. Sforza died at this time; and it is said that terror at the approach of the French, from whom his family and himself had undergone so many evils, hastened or produced the distemper of which he expired.

Meanwhile Charles, victorious from the capture of Tunis, and crowned with trophies gained over the Moors, prepared to revenge the injuries done to the duke of Savoy. After having given vent to his indignation against Francis, by an harangue in the conclave, filled with accusations and complaints of his perfidy and ambition, he joined his general Antonio de Leyva, so renowned for his great military exploits, and began the campaign. His victory in Africa; the servile flatteries of his courtiers and parasites; joined to the predictions of astrologers and fortune-tellers, who were then in no small estimation even with the wisest princes; had so inflated his vanity, and perverted an under-

understanding naturally cool, fagacious, and difcerning, that, in oppofition to the entreaties of his oldeft captains, he determined to enter Provence. Every argument and motive urged to diffuade him, were ineffectual. Blinded to reafons the moft cogent and forcible; untaught by Bourbon's experience and ill fuccefs; he paffed the river Var, and continued his march.

The king's wifdom and provident care were never more ably exerted, than in this imminent neceffity. Diftruftful of fortune, and cautious from the remembrance of paft difafters, he refolved to truft no event to the uncertain fate of battle; but to embrace a plan more circumfpect and prudent. To enfure the fafety of his kingdom, he facrificed a fingle province; and anticipated the ravages of the Imperial forces, by laying wafte, and totally deftroying the country through which he knew they muft pafs. Himfelf encamped at Valence, and prepared to try the iffue

KINGS OF FRANCE, &c. 255

of a second combat, in case Montmorenci, vanquished in a first, rendered it necessary for the general safety.

But while these public duties engrossed the attention of the King, a stroke of the most calamitous nature befel the Parent. The dauphin, his eldest son, a prince of the highest expectations, and peculiarly dear to his father, and to France, expired at nineteen years of age. The circumstances of his death, suspicious, and indicative of poison, encreased his sorrow and affliction. He had been engaged at tennis, in the meadow of Ainay near Lyons; and having violently heated himself by the exercise, dispatched one of his pages to draw him some water. Donna Agnes Beatrix Pacheco, a lady of honour in the service of the queen, had presented him with a curious cup made of earth, which gave a remarkable coolness to any liquor poured into it. While the page laid down this cup on the side of the well, and was employed in pulling up the bucket,

bucket, a certain Italian of Ferrara, by birth a nobleman, named Sebaſtian Montecuculi, approached, and unperceived mixed poiſon in the vaſe; which the dauphin immediately drank. He was ſeized with inſtant and moſt excruciating pains; but being warmly deſirous to embrace his father before his death, and to breathe his laſt in his arms, he cauſed himſelf to be put into a boat on the Rhone, in hopes of reaching the city of Valence alive: but even this little conſolation was not reſerved for his unhappy parent. The dauphin died, before he could reach him, at Tournon. Francis's magnanimity and fortitude ſunk beneath ſo cruel and diſaſtrous a trial; and it was long before he recovered in any degree his wonted ſerenity. Henry, his ſecond ſon, was not equally dear to him with the one he had loſt. If we may credit the cotemporary hiſtorians, he poſſeſſed many of thoſe qualities which conciliate admiration and love. In his perſon, he was handſome,

KINGS OF FRANCE, &c.

and formed with symmetry. His temper, serious, steady, and reserved, seemed to indicate an understanding more ripe and mature than his years gave reason to expect: and his deportment at the interview of Marseilles, impressed with respect and wonder, that numerous and august assembly.

Montecuculi was arrested, and confessed the crime. Under the violence of torture, he even accused Antonio de Leyva of being his accomplice, and threw out some dark and enigmatical insinuations against the emperor himself: but these imputations are too palpably false and unworthy to admit of a moment's belief, and were merely extorted from the agony of pain. He was himself executed, and torn in pieces by wild horses, at Lyons. The duke of Orleans succeeded to the title of dauphin, and left his own to Charles, the king's youngest son *.

Charles

* Notwithstanding the general testimony of historians, there appears to be a great uncertainty spread over

Charles purſuing his rout through Provence, during this ſad cataſtrophe, plundered the city of Aix, and ſat down before Marſeilles. At the end of a few weeks he found, when too late, the juſtice of thoſe remonſtrances which had been made him previous to his expedition. Antonio de Leyva had already breathed his laſt, killed by the ſame diſtemper which had carried off Lautrec before Naples. His troops became the prey of a thouſand diſeaſes incident to camps, and no proſpect appeared of the ſurrender of Marſeilles. Yielding to neceſſity, and compelled by theſe accumu-

---

over this whole tranſaction. Monteçuculi impeached the Imperial generals : the French writers have not ſcrupled to name, and with more probability, Catherine of Medicis, as the perpetrator of the dauphin's murder, in the view of advancing her huſband to the throne : but even this ſuppoſition ought not to be embraced without ſtronger reaſons. Poiſon is uſually attributed to the ſudden exits of diſtinguiſhed perſonages; and the ſymptoms of the dauphin's diſeaſe and death might have all been produced by drinking cold water, after an exerciſe which had exceedingly heated his blood.

lated

lated difasters which every day encreased, he began his march back into Savoy. All the roads were filled with his expiring soldiers; who, unable to support the fatigue of so unfortunate and painful a retreat, and incapable of accompanying their commander, dropped under the weight of their arms, and fell into the hands of the enemy.—Montmorenci, carrying his maxims of timid circumspection to an unjustifiable length, remained still in his camp near Avignon; and, instead of following an army dismayed and broken by toils, suffered them to escape, and repass the mountains.

Charles, covered with confusion, and desirous to hide his shame, remained only a short time in Italy. He embarked on his gallies at Genoa; and arriving, after a dreadful tempest, in Spain, buried himself in the recesses of his palace.

Mindful of the ancient alliances between the two crowns, and moved by the critical situation of France, menaced with so terrible an invasion, James the fifth, king of Scotland, flew to the assistance of Francis. He came too late for any actual service, the emperor being already on his retreat. This proof of generous and enthusiastic attachment so deeply touched the king, that he could not refuse him the boon he demanded; his daughter Magdalen. The princess was in the bloom of youth, beautiful, and accomplished : her ambition, gratified by a throne, induced her to accept with joy the proposal, though every endeavour was used to instil into her an aversion to it. The nuptials were celebrated at Paris, and the young queen accompanied her husband into his kingdom; but a hectic fever, with which she was seized soon after her arrival, put an end to her life, within a year from the marriage *. James,

become

---

* Brantome plainly indicates that her death was caused by sorrow and mortification, at having sacrificed her own delicious country to the ambition of

reigning

become a widower, and perſiſting in his
deſire of being connected with France,
received from the king, Mary of Guiſe
in ſecond marriage.

The war was ſtill continued with alternate ſucceſs in Flanders and Piedmont:
but the apparent intereſt which Francis
took in the affairs of Scotland, and the
two ſucceſſive unions with its ſovereign,
gave a jealouſy to Henry the eighth, and
gradually detached him from the ſtrict
cordiality he had long profeſſed for him.

Montmorenci poſſeſſed at this time an
influence the moſt extenſive and unbounded : he concentered in himſelf almoſt all

reigning in a rude and barbarous kingdom. When convinced by ſad experience of this truth, and conſcious
that her deſtiny permitted her to return no more, ſhe
funk under it, frequently exclaiming, " Helas ! j'ai
voulu etre reine !" Ronſard, the famous poet, has
celebrated the nuptials, and very minutely deſcribed
them in a ſort of epithalamium, not inelegant. He
was at that time a page to the duke of Orleans, who
preſented him to the queen at her departure, and he
accompanied her into Scotland.

the great powers of the royalty. To the fword of conftable, and grand mafter of the houfehold, was fuperadded the fovereign difpofal of the finances. Neither his talents or amiable qualities feem to have been fuch, as rendered him worthy of thefe unparalleled and diftinguifhed favours; and we are furprifed to find a man uniformly unfortunate in war, and interefted or partial in the cabinet, the minifter and moft beloved companion of two kings.—His ignorance was extreme, in an age and court where letters were peculiarly honoured and cultivated. His manners, brutal and ferocious, difgufted all who approached him. A temper ftern, imperious, unfeeling, rendered him generally odious and dreaded. Courage, loyalty, and adulation cannot be denied him. Francis, naturally difcerning, and capable, when not biaffed by paffion, of forming a juft eftimate of the human heart and mind, did not always continue to him that friendfhip and confidence.

He

He difgraced, and never would recall or employ him; but neither his conduct or advice could prevent his fon from extending to him the fame, or even greater honours, which continued without diminution till his death.

In the wifh or pretence of inducing Charles and Francis to a final peace, Paul the third, who had fucceeded to the pontificate, prevailed on both monarchs to agree to an interview at Nice. They came; but from uncertain motives, either perfonal or political, did not fee each other. The pope, who affected to perform the office of a mediator, could only procure a truce of nine years: but the emperor, at his departure, promifed to meet the king at Aigues-Mortes in Languedoc. He came, at the inftances of his fifter Eleanor; and landing without guards or precaution, waited on his rival, and dined in his tent. The enfuing day Francis returned this mark of confidence by a vifit to Charles; and was regaled on board his galley. Every demonſtration of mutual eſteem and friendſhip was interchanged. They embraced, and appeared to have obliterated all their paſt animoſities. —But the emperor, deeply ſkilled in the ſubtle mazes of policy, and well acquainted with the character of the king, generous, and, when piqued on his honour, carrying his punctilio to an extreme, foreſaw that he ſhould have occaſion to requeſt a paſſage through his dominions; and only wore the ſemblance of amity and concord, to deceive the more eaſily and effectually.

On his return from this interview, Francis, who paſſionately loved the ſtudy of nature, and poſſeſſed a curioſity of the moſt elegant and liberal kind, gratified himſelf by ſeveral reſearches which mark his turn of mind, and are not uſual in princes. He made a journey into Dauphiné, a province rich in romantic and ſingular beauties; in phænomena of various ſpecies. He even cauſed a boat to be conſtructed for the purpoſe of exploring a
ſubterranean

subterranean lake, near a village called Notre Dame de la Baulme, on the road from Grenoble to Lyons; and having ventured into it, proceeded a confiderable diftance on the water: but a strong current, which grew more rapid as they advanced, attended with a noise indicative of a whirlpool, obliged his guides to defist from a farther progress, and to reconduct him to the entrance of the grotto *.

Francis, who had already sacrificed his first queen to his irregular pleasures, experienced in turn the fatal effects of his indiscretion; and was eventually a martyr to the most cruel of all diseases. He became enamoured of a woman, known un-

---

* This story is inconteftably authentic, and occurs in almost all the French historians. I have omitted many circumstances of it, as being too minute. The remains of a boat, said to be that of Francis the first, were yet to be feen some few years since, in the cavern, through which is the passage to the lake. The " Sept merveilles de Dauphiné," are well known, and are yet visited by the curious.

der

der the name of "La belle Feroniere," in hiftory. Her rank and condition are fomewhat uncertain. Confcious how dangerous it is to oppofe the paffions or defires of princes, her hufband pretended to fubmit to his own difhonour: but nourifhing the refolution of vengeance, and unable to devife any other expedient, he voluntarily contracted a diftemper, which he communicated to his unhappy wife, and fhe, unknowingly, to the king. The hufband adminiftered quick and effectual remedies to his complaint; but "La Fe-
" roniere" furvived it only a fhort time. Even Francis, whether from unfkilful treatment in his phyficians, or neglect, never perfectly recovered this fingular punifhment. He underwent extreme pain from its effects; and, after dragging on feven or eight years of life, under a continual return of fymptoms more and more alarming, expired in the vigour of his age; a melancholy leffon of the dreadful confequences of debauchery, and a proof that

that no exaltation of dignity can preclude revenge, or shield from jealous indignation *.

But though these were the pernicious attendants on his incontinence, yet was it productive of certain intermediate benefits to the kingdom. Pain and mental anxiety acting constantly on him, gradually affected and changed his disposition. No longer capable of pursuing, as formerly, his appetites, unrestrained, and compelled to a life more temperate and prudent; he renounced his profusion, and became sparing of the re-

* Every writer of Francis's reign relates this extraordinary anecdote; and it is found, though with some unessential variation in minute particulars, in Mezerai, Varillas, Le Calendrier du Pere L'Enfant, Louis Guyon, Bussieres, Bayle, and many others.—The portrait of " La belle Feroniere" is yet to be seen in cabinets, and forms one of the beauties in the famous collection of Odieuvre. The most common opinion is, that her husband was a lawyer; but that is not certain.——I think Dr. Burnet relates a similar story of James the second, when duke of York.

venues.

venues. Favourites, used to the abuse of his bounty, lost their command over him. He applied more seriously to the great business of state; and, becoming splenetic, inaccessible, and reserved, introduced order through all the departments of government.

The rebellion of the inhabitants of Ghent, which took place at this time, served to oppose, in the most striking and eminent point of view, the different genius and character of Charles and Francis. So far was the latter from taking advantage of their insurrection, and offers of submission to him, that he even gave advice of it to the emperor; and granted him a passage through his dominions, without laying him, as he might have done, under any conditions, except those of gratitude and honour. Every attention of the most profound respect, of the most disinterested friendship, was lavishly heaped upon him. The dauphin and duke of Orleans, accompanied by the constable, went to receive him at Bayonne, and even

offered

KINGS OF FRANCE, &c. 269

offered to go as hoſtages into Spain for the ſecurity of his perſon. The king himſelf, though exceedingly indiſpoſed by illneſs, advanced as far as Chatelleraud in Poictou, where they gave each other all the marks of eſteem and amity at their rencontre. Honours more than regal were ſhewn him; all orders of the ſtate vied in their endeavours to welcome his arrival, and to heighten the ſplendor of his entry into the capital.

It was debated in the cabinet, to improve the occaſion, and to compel the emperor by force, if not by benefits, to the reſtitution of the Milaneſe, which he had engaged himſelf by a verbal promiſe to do, previous to his entry into the kingdom. Montmorenci alone declared againſt the general ſentiment: and, whether influenced by Charles's applauſes, who flattered and careſſed him to the greateſt degree; whether induced to give this counſel from an attachment to the queen Eleanor, or from motives yet more uncertain and concealed;

S   prevailed

prevailed on Francis, eafily led to comply with the dictates of his native dignity of foul, and fcorning the arts of a fordid policy, to lay him under no reftriction. He even conducted himfelf towards the emperor with a delicacy unexampled; accompanied him, on his departure, to St. Quintin, and fent his two fons to attend him to Valenciennes. Thefe accumulated favours were repaid with the meaneft breach of his word, with fubterfuges and evafions too low for repetition. Charles, who never meant to refign the rich duchy of Milan, and only fought to deceive a rival too honourable for the crooked line of princely conduct, avowed his intention when he no longer feared reprifals; and, like his grandfather Ferdinand, did not blufh at a fuccefsful perfidy *.

The

* There is a curious anecdote on the fubject of Charles's paffage through France, and efcape, in Dupleix; who attributes it almoft entirely to the duchefs of Eftampes. Francis, in prefenting his mif-

trefs

The indignation, mixed with shame, which the king felt at being thus egregiously the dupe of his too scrupulous and unsuspecting honour, roused him from that supine reliance on the counsel of others, which he had hitherto indulged. His penetration made him see, that treachery in his own servants, had been added to the emperor's duplicity, and

tress to the emperor, said, "Mon frere, cette belle dame
" me conseille de vous obliger à detruire à Paris l'ou-
" vrage de Madrid;" to which he coldly replied, " Si
" le conseil en est bon, il faut le suivre." Alarmed
however at this intimation of the duchess's sentiments,
and conscious of her power over the king, he determined to exert his whole address to detach her from
him. On the ensuing day, when water was offered
him to wash, Madame d'Estampes held the napkin. In
pulling off a diamond of prodigious value, which he
wore on his finger, he purposely let it drop; and she
having taken it up, Charles refused to accept it, adding gallantly, that it too well became the hand where
fortune had placed it, to take it away. The duchess
was too grateful for the present.——There is an air of
fiction and romance in all this, nor can it be much
relied on; though it is but too clear that she had intelligence with Charles, in the sequel.

jointly

jointly impofed on his underftanding. As he carried his infpection deeper into the arcana of adminiftration, new proofs of the pernicious abufe which his favourites had made of the royal ear or affection, crouded upon him. Pleafure, feductive and fafcinating, had ceafed to delude his ripened judgment; the cares and duties of a great monarch, anxious for the public weal, fucceeded to their empire in his bofom; and the fhining virtues which nature had early planted there, but whofe growth had been retarded, and luftre dimmed, by a too early acceffion to the crown, rekindled in an age lefs fufceptible of flattery.

This alteration of fentiment was followed by as total a change of action. The perfons to whom the firft offices and charges had been confided, were difgraced. Brion, admiral of France, was degraded from his high poft; and though the interceffion of the duchefs of Eftampes, to whom he was allied by blood, alleviated the feverity

KINGS OF FRANCE, &c. 273

verity of his profecution and fentence, yet he died the victim of his mortified pride, and humbled fortunes. Poyet, the chancellor, was the fecond facrifice; and his punifhment, more rigorous and extenfive, reduced him to penury and extreme diftrefs. His conduct while he held the feals, no lefs reproachable than Du Prat's, his predeceffor, deprived him, in this calamitous condition, of the popular commiferation. Thefe two confpicuous removals only ferved to prepare a yet greater fall, that of the conftable, fo long unrivalled in Francis's love. The caufe cannot be exactly afcertained, nor can we even pofitively know whether it was more political, or perfonal. It is faid, that a jealoufy of the dauphin's growing attachment to him, gave umbrage to his father, and ferved to corroborate the other reafons I have enumerated. Montmorenci retired from court, and amufed himfelf in the erection of the caftle of Ecoüen, near St. Denis, during his exile;

nor could the king ever be perfuaded to recal or employ him, by any inftances or endeavours for that purpofe. The cardinal of Tournon, a man of mediocrity of talents, but poffeffing application, and capacity for bufinefs, was invefted with the higheft employment of ftate; and the marechal d'Annebaut, who fucceeded Brion as admiral, divided with him the king's confidence.

After near two years of intrigue, negociation, and infidious propofals on the part of the emperor, relative to the pretended refignation of the Milanefe in favour of Charles duke of Orleans; Francis, confcious that thefe meafures would never produce the end intended, and irritated by the marquis del Guafto's murder of his two ambaffadors to the republic of Venice and Solyman emperor of the Turks, openly took up arms, and renewed the war. He even made efforts of a nature more extraordinary than any during his whole reign. Henry, the dauphin,

phin, was placed at the head of a fine army in the Roufillon, and laid fiege to Perpignan; but after a vain attempt, was neceffitated to retire without fuccefs. His brother Charles, after a much more profperous campaign in Flanders, abandoned his triumphs in the midway; and, inflamed with the wifh to combat the emperor, who was expected to come to the refcue of Perpignan, quitted his troops, and croffed all France to Montpelier, where his father had remained, to wait the event. Scarce any advantageous confequences refulted from thefe great armaments.

Francis gave at this time an inftance of the moft amiable clemency, in his treatment of the inhabitants of La Rochelle, who had revolted. After having entered with a great military train into the city, which was incapable of defence, and expofed to his refentment; he firft pointed out to them, in an eloquent harangue, the enormity of their crime, and then pardoned

pardoned it, without reftriction, in the moft ample manner.

The king of England, capricious, and the fport of his tumultuous paffions, had once more broke with Francis, and renewed his ancient alliance with his rival. The Netherlands became the fcene of hoftilities; and, though incommoded from illnefs, he was neceffitated to command his forces in perfon. Luxembourg was taken, but no conqueft of importance atchieved.

Induced by the preffing folicitations of the king, Solyman the magnificent difpatched the renowned pirate Barbaroffa, with a hundred and thirty gallies, to his aid: in conjunction with the French fleet, he laid fiege to Nice, but raifed it difhonourably; and Francis, covered with the reproaches of all the chriftian princes, for this union with their common enemy, derived from it fcarce any benefit or utility. In Flanders he was more fuccefsful: Charles, who had led a formidable

army

army into the field, was repulfed before Landrecy, by the valour of the garrifon; and after having feized on Cambray, an imperial city, retired into winter quarters.

After ten years of fterility, Catherine of Medecis was at length delivered of a fon, who was named Francis, and afterwards afcended the throne. Her character had not yet unveiled and difplayed itfelf: the genius of Francis, and the circumftances of the times, repreffed and concealed it. She poffeffed no political influence, had no feat in the cabinet. Her barrennefs contributed to diminifh her confequence, and even gave room to fome propofals for a diffolution of the marriage, but which were relinquifhed. Even in this fituation, her addrefs was vifible: fhe made the moft affiduous and fuccefsful court to the king, who began to decline, from his indifpofitions: fhe accompanied him to the chace; formed one of that celebrated party, known by the title of

"La

"La petite bande de dames de la cour;" and attended him on his private excurſions to Chambord, Fontainbleau, and Madrid, where he laid aſide the cares of ſtate, and unbent himſelf in the company of a ſelect number of his favourites. Theſe complaiſant and winning attentions, rendered her infinitely dear to Francis.—To her huſband, the dauphin, ſhe was no leſs ſubmiſſive: he was already enſlaved to Diana de Poitiers, whoſe faction, oppoſed to that of madame d'Eſtampes, divided the court. In this moſt delicate and critical condition, ſhe yet rendered herſelf acceptable by a humility and flexibility of conduct rarely found; and, reſerving the latent capacities with which ſhe was endowed for more favourable times, was content to remain in comparative obſcurity *.

The

---

* Though certain authors have ſpoken of the "Petite bande de dames de la cour," as a moſt diſſolute and voluptuous aſſociation, yet there can be no
doubt

The war between the two monarchs was carried on with redoubled violence. Francis had confided the fupreme command in Piedmont to the count d'Enguien. This young hero, only twenty-one years of age, had already raifed the higheft expectations: in him revived the genius of Gafton de Foix; and, like him, his glories were fwallowed up by a hafty extinction. Brother to Anthony duke of Vendome, and to Louis prince of Condé fo renowned in the unhappy wars of Charles the ninth, his rank entitled him to the higheft employments, and his capacity

---

doubt of the falfity of fuch an accufation. It is likewife faid, that Catherine prevented a divorce between Henry and herfelf, by the intereft of Diana de Poitiers, his miftrefs, of which fhe did not fcruple to make ufe; but this is very problematical, and much to be difputed. Uniform tradition, and feveral cotemporary writers, attribute to Fernel, firft phyfician to the king, the merit of rendering her capable of bearing children, by fome medical affiftance given to her conftitution; and there feems every reafon to believe it.

made him worthy of them. The battle of Cerizoles, which he gained over the marquis del Guafto, who fled, wounded in the knee, renewed the remembrance of Ravenna's day. All the Milanefe would have been the inevitable confequence of this important victory, if urgent neceffity had not compelled the king to renounce Italian conquefts, in the more preffing exigence of domeftic invafion. Charles and Henry entering Picardy with two great armies, menaced France with calamities fuperior to any fhe had yet experienced. Had the junction been made which was originally ftipulated, the kingdom would probably have been reduced to the verge of ruin : but the emperor's error in laying fiege to St. Difier, which detained him more than fix weeks—and the king of England's refufal to join him, or defift from his attempt on Boulogne—gave Francis time to provide for the fafety of his capital and dominions. He was himfelf too much enfeebled by his complaints,

to

to head the army in perſon; which was intruſted to the dauphin. The emperor advancing, ſpread terror and conſternation. Paris, abandoned by its inhabitants, was left almoſt unpeopled, and preſented a ſcene the moſt diſtreſsful: ſcarce could the king's arrival calm their agitations, and reſtore any ſort of tranquillity.

Meanwhile his ſon Henry, active, martial, and warmed with enthuſiaſm in ſo great a cauſe, had reduced Charles, in turn, to the greateſt difficulties for want of forage and proviſions. He muſt even, it is probable, have ſued for a ceſſation of arms, or made a difficult and ſhameful retreat; if the intrigues of the duchefs of Eſtampes had not extricated him from his perilous ſituation, by a private information of thoſe places where magazines were provided. The motive to this infamous and treaſonable conduct in the king's miſtreſs, was her jealouſy of the dauphin's glory, and partiality for the

the duke of Orleans; to whom she hoped Charles would resign the Milanese, and under whose protection she flattered herself with a secure asylum after Francis's death. Though her succour had prevented his troops from being destroyed by famine, yet many circumstances hung the fortune of the campaign in suspence: and Henry, panting to signalize his prowess, and shew himself worthy the crown he was destined to inherit, might still have snatched from him the trophies he had gained.—These considerations prevailed on the emperor to propose, or permit the proposal, of a final peace. Two Dominican friars, Diegos Chiavez, and Gabriel de Gusman, were the conductors of this negotiation, which was warmly seconded by Eleanor, Francis's queen. The dauphin, on the other hand, strongly and violently opposed it, as inglorious, unnecessary, and a sacrifice of the national honour to the aggrandisement of his brother, the only object intended by the contrary

trary faction. The king, after some irresolution, ranged himself on the side of his youngest son, for whom he indulged a partial fondness.—The treaty was, in consequence, less calculated for public benefit, than that of the duke of Orleans, to whom the emperor promised his daughter, with the Low Countries or Milanese in dowry, within two years. A contingent and future advantage; in return for which Francis resigned almost all his conquests in Savoy or Piedmont; and which Charles never accomplished!— Henry the dauphin protested publicly against this treaty, so injurious to his interests.

The capture of Boulogne, which had fallen into the king of England's hands, had served to hasten its conclusion; and Francis, anxious for the recovery of so important a place, not only sent his eldest son to form the siege of it, but advanced in person, accompanied by his youngest, to the abbey of Foret-Moustier, ten

leagues

leagues diftant, between Abbeville and Montreuil. Here he was again overwhelmed by a new affliction, to which he was infinitely fenfible; the death of the duke of Orleans. This prince was the unhappy victim of his own puerile temerity and want of confideration. The plague had appeared in the environs of the village where the king was lodged: his fon, notwithftanding the entreaties and remonftrances of his attendants, perfifted to fleep in a houfe faid to be infected; alledging, that in the annals of the monarchy was there no inftance of a fon of France who had died of the plague. He even carried his fatal indifcretion to a yet more extraordinary length; and having pulled out the bedding faid to be tainted, ran up and down covered with the feathers. He was feized almoft immediately with the diftemper predicted, and expired foon after. His unfortunate parent fainted at the mournful news of the lofs of this favourite child, for whom he had with

fo

KINGS OF FRANCE, &c. 285

so much care provided a rich inheritance.

The duke of Orleans was only twenty-three years old: in person he resembled Francis more than either of his elder sons, and was the handsomest of his three children. He had no bodily defect, except that the small-pox had injured one of his eyes; but even this was not discernible. As the features of his face bore a peculiar similarity to those of his father, so did the leading strokes of his character. Lively, animated, courageous, active, and incapable of disguise or reserve: but with those errors and foibles which commonly characterize youth; presumption, warmth, and vanity. He was doubtless a prince of high expectations, if the rivalship and avowed animosity between him and the dauphin had not rendered it too probable, that after Francis's death the brothers would no longer preserve any measures. The emperor fomented this disunion; and, by an affected predilection

for

for, and preference of him, inſtilled deeper ſuſpicions into Henry's boſom; ſo that perhaps his untimely end was not injurious to the ſtate, however calamitous and oppreſſive to the father.—Charles immediately declared, that by this accident he held himſelf acquitted from his promiſe relative to the Milaneſe; and refuſed any reſignation or inveſtiture of it.

The death of the count d'Enguien, who had ſo lately acquired an immortal renown in Italy, and whoſe age was almoſt exactly the ſame with that of the prince deceaſed, renewed the grief of Francis, who wept his loſs in the deepeſt ſorrow. There is an ambiguity ſpread over this event, hard to penetrate. The count was engaged at play with the youth of the court. It was at La Roche-ſur-Yonne: a coffer thrown purpoſely from a window on his head, killed him on the ſpot. Cornelio Bentivoglio, an Italian nobleman, with whom he previouſly had ſome diſpute, was accuſed of this deteſtable

and

and cowardly action: but the king would not permit the affair to be minutely examined, or any difquifition entered into, from the fear of finding that the dauphin was privy to, or involved in the crime.

A peace, long wifhed for by the two kings of France and England, at length took place. Henry promifed to reftore Boulogne in eight years, on condition of a certain annual fum; and Francis, releafed from this object of attention, bent all his cares to the empire, where Charles had openly attempted to eftablifh an unlimited power.

As he approached the termination of his life, the violence of the two parties, which divided the court, redoubled. The duchefs of Eftampes had endeavoured to fpread a report, that Diana de Poitiers was the caufe of the duke of Orleans's death, by the adminiftration of poifon. To this cruel imputation, fhe had added many contemptuous expreffions on the decay of her perfonal charms; and openly declared, that

that the year of Diana's marriage was that of her own birth. The dauphin, in revenge for thefe afperfions on his miftrefs's fame, had indulged himfelf in fome very fevere and pointed farcafms on the duchefs's fidelity. He even prefumed to affert, that fhe confoled herfelf for his father's ficknefs in the arms of another; and he named the celebrated Guy Chabot, Seigneur de Jarnac, as the perfon, tho' he was nearly allied to her, having married her fifter. This accufation reached the king's ear, who highly refented it, and would have rigoroufly punifhed the author, had not his name been concealed. Jarnac denied the fact; which La Chataigneraye, a favourite of the dauphin's, protefted he had communicated to him; and from this fource originated. the famous duel which took place on Henry the fecond's acceffion *.

We

* It was not only with Jarnac, that madame d'Eftampes has been accufed of infidelity. The count de
Boffu,

We draw towards the clofe of this great reign. Henry the eighth of England's death alarmed and difquieted the king; he had long known him, and a degree of diftant analogy and refemblance in their characters, had united them to each other, in defiance of their frequent wars and jarring interefts. Francis caufed a re-

Boffu, and the Seigneur de Dampierre, have been likewife named; but none of thefe are proved, and probably only originated from the dauphin and his miftrefs's hatred. Even Brantome, partial to his uncle La Chataigneraie, only infinuates, that the duchefs was not ftrictly faithful to Francis, as he did not pique himfelf on his fidelity to her. It was not her perfonal, but political conduct, which rendered her obnoxious to Henry; who, after his father's death, protefted againft the abufe which fhe had made of her influence over him, and aided publicly the profecution againft her.—There have been authors fo abfurd as to pretend, that Francis never had any other connections with her than thofe of mind, during two-and-twenty years: it would be ridiculous to attempt to difprove this formally. The complexion of the king, amorous and warm; the beauty, and many attractions of the duchefs, refute it fufficiently.

quiem and service to be said for the repose of his soul, though he died excommunicated, and without the pale of the church. He considered it as a prognostic of his own approaching end, and was deeply affected by it. No effectual remedies could be administered to his disease, which was grown inveterate: his uneasiness and anxiety of mind encreased its virulence. He wandered from one palace to another, depressed and languid. A slow fever, produced by corporal and intellectual pain, began to waste his already exhausted constitution; and at length, becoming more violent and continued, forced him to stop at the little chateau of Rambouillet. Here, finding himself worse, and resigning the hope of life, he sent for his son Henry, that he might address to him his dying words. They were worthy a great king expiring.——He admonished him, that children should imitate the virtues, and not the vices of their parents; that the French people, as the most loyal and liberal

beral of any in the world to their fovereigns, merited in return to be protected, not oppreffed by them. He recommended to him, in terms the moft forcible and perfuafive, the diminution of the impofts and taxes, which continual wars had forced him to encreafe to an unprecedented heighth. He requefted him never to recall Montmorenci; and to continue the cardinal of Tournon, and the marechal d'Annebaut in the miniftry, as virtuous and difinterefted ftatefmen. Henry fhewed little deference to thefe counfels, when he afcended the throne. His father did not furvive much longer: the perfect poffeffion of his underftanding and fpeech accompanied him to the laft moment: he expired at length, aged only fifty-two years, of which he had reigned thirty-two. The magnificence which had diftinguifhed him through life, did not forfake him even in death: his funeral obfequies were performed with unufual pomp,

pomp, and attended by eleven cardinals: a thing unprecedented in France!

I have been irresistibly and insensibly drawn into too minute a narration of Francis's reign, to render it necessary to be equally diffuse in the description of his character. Such are the principal strokes of it, that they cannot be mistaken. We shall love and admire his magnanimity, his clemency, his munificence, his romantic and scrupulous honour. We shall confess and respect his capacity, his courage, his protection of genius and the arts, his heroism and fortitude.—We shall pity, and hide beneath the veil of candour and humanity, his profusion, his want of application, his too great subserviency to ministers, favourites, and mistresses, who abused his bounty.—No prince of the age in which he lived, interests so deeply; none was so much celebrated, and the subject of such universal panegyric. Though usually unsuccesful in his wars, he yet acquired

quired more glory than the emperor his competitor; and Francis is more truly great after the defeat of Pavia, or in the caftle of Madrid, than Charles triumphant, and impofing conditions on his prifoner. His largeffes, his princely liberality, his condefcending attentions to men diftinguifhed by their fuperior merit, acquired him a fame not inferior to Leo the tenth, and lefs oftentatious than that of Louis the fourteenth. We all know that Leonardo-da-Vinci expired in his arms, from the effort he made to exprefs his fenfe of the honours done him by fo auguft a monarch.

No European court vied with that of Francis in brilliance and luftre. He was himfelf the animating foul, which diffufed a radiance over it.—During the laft ten years of his life, his character rifes upon the view. Notwithftanding all the previous diforder in the finances, notwithftanding the numerous and fplendid palaces he erected, the donations he made, the collections of paintings and other monuments of art which he purchafed, the inceffant wars he fuftained; yet at his death the royal domain was free, a vaft fum in the treafury, and a quarter of his revenues ready to enter it.—His very foibles and errors were fuch as mark a feeling and generous bofom; fuch as we pardon while we cenfure. His promifcuous amours carried with them their own punifhment, and conducted him to the tomb untimely, before age had diminifhed his faculties or powers. To Henry the fourth he bears a ftriking refemblance; and this latter prince, fo worthy of immortal praife, was flattered and charmed with the comparifon of himfelf to Francis, whom he imitated and emulated. The proclamation in the hall of the palace, which announced his death, was couched in thefe words: " Prince clement en paix, victorieux en " guerre, pere et reftaurateur des bonnes " lettres, et des arts liberaux." An eulogium great and dazzling, but yet far unequal,

unequal, in real and intrinfic dignity, to that conferred on his predeceffor! By Eleanor, his fecond wife, he never had any iffue; and on his deceafe fhe retired firft into the Netherlands, and afterwards into Spain; in which country fhe died, at Talavera, near Badajox, eleven years after her hufband. We know not that Francis had any children by either of his moft celebrated miftreffes, madame de Chateau-Briand, and the duchefs of Eftampes *.

* Brantome has mentioned a certain " Villecou- "vin," as his illegitimate fon; but this is very dubious.—It is curious to find in the Jefuit Garaffe, and in Sanderus, that Anne Boleyn is accufed of having been one of Francis's miftreffes. They not only vilify her character by invectives the moft illiberal; but defcribe her perfon in language fo extraordinary, that I cannot help copying it from the latter of thefe writers.—" Anne de Boleyn avoit fix " doigts à la main droite; le vifage long, jaune, " comme fi elle eut eu les pales couleurs; et une " loupe fous la gorge."—Is this the beautiful Anne Boleyn? It is at leaft impoffible to recognize her under thefe frightful and ridiculous colours.

CHAPTER THE EIGHTH.

Character of Henry the second.—Changes in the state.—Diana de Poitiers.—Her character.—Romantic attachment of the king.—Disgrace of the duchess of Estampes.—Duel of Jarnac and La Chataigneraie.—Insurrections in Guyenne.—Persecution of the protestants.—Death of Margaret of Valois, queen of Navarre,—Character.—War renewed between Henry and the Emperor.—Catherine of Medicis left regent.—Siege of Metz.—War continued.—The Emperor abdicates,—Power of Diana duchess of Valentinois.—The duke of Guise sent against Naples.—Battle of St. Quentin.—Capture of Calais.—Marriage of Francis the dauphin, to Mary of Scotland.—Circumstances,— Peace concluded.—Carousals of the court.—The king's unexpected death.— Enumeration

of

of the circumstances which attended it.—Character of Henry the second.—Mistresses.—Reflections.

THOUGH the death of so great a prince as Francis the first, at a period of life when his character promised happiness and tranquillity to his people, was an event deeply to be lamented by those to whom the interests of the state were dear; yet as his successor had attained to years of manhood, and did not appear to be deficient in the qualities requisite for government, his loss might be deemed not irreparable.

Henry the second, who ascended the throne, was the handsomest monarch of his age, and the most accomplished cavalier in his dominions. He surpassed in all the martial exercises where vigour and address are necessary; and bore away the prize in tournaments with distinguished grace. His heart was beneficent and humane; his temper courteous, open, and liberal.

liberal. His intentions were ever honourable, and directed to the public good; but he neither poffeffed the capacity or difcernment which Francis eminently difcovered: and, naturally tractable, and yielding to others, was formed to be under the guidance of favourites.

His father's dying exhortations had made no impreffion on his heart, produced no effect on his conduct. Scarce were his funeral rites performed, when he violated them in every point. Montmorenci, who had been during feveral years in difgrace, was recalled, and loaded with honours. The admiral d'Annebaut was difmiffed, and the cardinal of Tournon only retained a fhadow of authority. In their place, Francis duke of Guife, fo celebrated in the fubfequent reigns, and the marechal de St. André, were fubftituted. That pernicious profufion, which had characterifed the commencement of the late king's government, was carried to a more unjuftifiable length; and the trea-

fures

sures amassed during his concluding years, were dissipated with a wanton extravagance.

Diana de Poitiers, who may be said to have divided the crown with her lover; and who carried her influence, personal and political, to a pitch which madame d'Estampes never could attain, was the directing principle of Henry's councils, the object of his tenderest attachment, and unlimited homage. This extraordinary woman, unparalleled in the annals of history, retained her beauty undiminished even in the autumn of life, and preserved her powers of enslaving, of fascinating, in defiance of time and natural decay. She was already forty-eight, while Henry had scarce attained his twenty-ninth year. Her father, John de Poitiers, Seigneur de St. Vallier, had been condemned to die as an accomplice in the revolt of the constable Charles of Bourbon; and though he escaped with life, yet he was degraded from the nobility, and all his fortunes confiscated.

confiscated *. She was married, in the last year of Louis the twelfth's reign, to Louis de Brezé, count de Maulevrier, and grand senechal of Normandy; by whom she had two daughters still alive. It is not certain when her connections with the dauphin first commenced; but it appears, that before he had completed his eighteenth year, her ascendancy over him was well established. All the cotemporary authors agree in their assurances, that her

* Mezerai, the president Henault, and many other writers, have asserted, that she was the instrument of her father's preservation, by the sacrifice of her chastity to Francis the first; from whose embraces she passed into those of his son: but this is very dubious, not to say certainly mistaken. She had been married near ten years at that time, and consequently had not, as those authors seem to imagine, her *virgin honour* to give. Besides, though her father's life was not taken, his punishment was commuted for another, worse than death; that of being immured perpetually between four walls, in which there should be only one little window, through which his provisions might be given him. St. Vallier died of a fever, produced by terror, in a very short time afterwards.'

charms

charms were of the moſt captivating kind, and worthy a monarch's love. To theſe corporal endowments, ſhe united a cultivated and juſt underſtanding, wit, and an animated converſation. Warmly devoted to her friends and partizans, ſhe was a dangerous and implacable enemy: of high and unſubmitting ſpirit, ſhe tranſfuſed thoſe ſentiments into the royal boſom, and impelled him to actions of vigour and firmneſs. Fond of power, ſhe was yet more ſo of flattery and ſubmiſſion. The nobles crouded to expreſs their dutiful attentions to this idol; and even the conſtable, rude, haughty, and more accuſtomed to inſult than flatter, bent beneath her, and condeſcended to ingratiate himſelf by the meaneſt adulation.

The tyes which chiefly bound Henry to her, were probably firſt thoſe of pleaſure and voluptuous enjoyment; and afterwards habit, taſte, and preſcription. In vain did the ducheſs of Eſtampes exert every art of female rivalry and hatred, to ſeparate

and

and difunite them: in vain did fhe publifh, that Diana was married in the fame year which gave herfelf birth.—Thefe efforts only encreafed the paffion they were defigned to extinguifh. The king carried it to an incredible and romantic length; he gave her every public, as well as private proof of her empire over him. The furniture of his palaces, his armour, the public edifices, were all diftinguifhed with her device and emblems; a moon, bow, and arrows. Every favour or preferment was obtained thro' her intereft; and Briffac, the moft amiable and gallant nobleman of the court, faid to be peculiarly acceptable to her, was created grand mafter of the artillery, at her particular requeft.—The Count de Boffu, who had been intimately connected with the late king's miftrefs, and was accufed of treafonable practices with the emperor, could only fhelter himfelf from punifhment by a refignation of his palace at Marchez to the cardinal of Lorain. The duchefs of Eftampes, unfupported

ported by the croud of flatterers who attended on her in Francis's reign, was neceffitated to quit the court;—but Diana, whether from motives of prudence or magnanimity, did not attempt to defpoil her of the poffeffions fhe had acquired from the late king's generofity. Difgraced, and forfaken, fhe retired to one of her country houfes, where fhe lived many years in total obfcurity *.

Henry having returned from a vifit which he made to the frontier of Picardy, not only permitted, but was prefent with all his courtiers at the celebrated duel between Jarnac and La Chataigneraie. It was decided at St. Germain-en-Laye. The quarrel had originated from the ac-

* It is fomewhat extraordinary, that the year of Madame d'Eftampes's death is not mentioned by any cotemporary author. All we know is, that fhe was yet alive in 1575, as fhe did homage at that time for one of her eftates. She became a protectrefs to the Lutherans or Hugonots, for whom fhe had always a concealed affection; and this is the only circumftance we are acquainted with of her retreat.

cufation

cufation of the latter refpecting Madame d'Eftampes's infidelity; and was increafed by a fecond imputation, ftill more difhonourable to Jarnac, that of having been criminally intimate with his father's fecond wife. La Chataigneraie was one of the moft accomplifhed cavaliers, and moft acceptable to the king, of any in his dominions. Skilled in the practice of arms, vain of his acknowledged addrefs, relying on the royal favour, and elated with fo many advantages, he defpifed his antagonift; and vaunted to his miftrefs, that he would prefent her a " Tete de " Chabot," alluding to Jarnac's family name. He, more cautious, and neither fupported by fuperior force, or ftimulated by the regal patronage, endeavoured to fupply thefe defects by artificial aid. A fever had diminifhed even his ufual ftrength and activity; but the prefumptuous negligence of La Chataigneraie decided the duel in his honour. By a ftroke totally unexpected, he wounded

him

him in the ham, and threw him to the ground. Henry inſtantly flung down his baton, to ſuſpend the engagement: Jarnac, as the law of arms required, defiſted; but his competitor, ſtung with diſappointment, covered with ſhame, and incapable of ſurviving theſe accumulated mortifications, would not accept of a life which he deemed ignominious; and having torn off the bandages applied to his wounds, expired ſoon after. The king was ſo deeply touched with this combat, and its event, ſo oppoſite to his wiſhes and expectations, that he made a ſolemn vow, never, during his reign, to permit a ſecond, on whatever pretext.

The ſources of future wars, unextinguiſhed by the death of Francis, began to generate between the emperor and Henry; though as yet many circumſtances conduced to retard and protract an open rupture. This latter prince made a progreſs through part of his dominions, attended with ſplendid entries into the principal cities; and on his return he celebrated the nuptials of Anthony duke of Vendome with Jane d'Albret, heirefs of the kingdom of Navarre, at the city of Moulins *.

A dan-

* The young princefs had been efpoufed feveral years before to the duke of Cleves. Francis the firſt was prefent at this ceremony, which was performed with great ſplendor at Chatelleraud in Poiƈtou: but the marriage was not confummated, on account of her extreme youth, ſhe being at that time little more than twelve years old. The day was rendered remarkable by the difmiffion and difgrace of the conſtable Montmorenci; which was preceded by a very fingular circumſtance, fuppofed to foretel his approaching fall. The bride, according to the manners of the age, was habited in robes fo weighty, and charged with many pearls and jewels, that not being able to move, Francis commanded the conſtable to take her in his arms, and carry her to the church. Though this cuſtom was uſual at the nuptials of great perfons, yet Montmorenci was deeply hurt by being feleƈted for fuch an office; and regarding it as an inconteſtible proof of his ruin, hefitated not to declare to his friends, that his favour was at an end. The event juſtified his fufpicion; for immediately after the banquet, the king difmiffed him from his fervice,

and

A dangerous infurrection, which broke out at this time in Guienne, rendering it neceſſary to ſend into the province ſome general of rank and experience, the duke of Guiſe, and the conſtable were both

and he quitted the court directly. Margaret of Valois, queen of Navarre, and mother to Jane d'Albret, was ſuppoſed, by her intereſt with her brother, to have accelerated his downfall. The conſtable had not ſcrupled to accuſe her to Francis, of being attached to, and protecting the Hugonots. By this imputation againſt his beloved ſiſter, he offended the king, and raiſed up an implacable and powerful enemy in Margaret herſelf.

The marriage of Jane with the duke of Cleves, which had been chiefly made in compliance with the wiſhes of Francis the firſt, was afterwards broken from motives of policy, on his death. But Brantome ſays, that Anthony duke of Vendome had great ſcruples of delicacy relative to eſpouſing the princeſs; and had recourſe to the ſenechale of Poictou, who was at the time of her firſt nuptials a lady of honour to the queen of Navarre, to clear up his ſuſpicions.—She did ſo; and gave him the moſt ſolemn and ſatisfactory proofs, that her firſt marriage had been merely a ceremony; to which, as reaſons of ſtate gave riſe, ſo oppoſite ones might equally diſſolve it at pleaſure.

charged

charged with that commiſſion. The former, courteous, humane, and paſſionately deſirous to conciliate popular favour, entered Saintonge and Angoumois, diſpenſing pardon, or only puniſhing with lenity and gentleneſs; but Montmorenci, ſtern, inexorable, and with a ſeverity of temper which approached to cruelty, marked his courſe along the Garonne with blood; and, deaf to the ſupplications of the inhabitants, who had recourſe to ſubmiſſions and deprecations, put to death above a hundred of the principal citizens of Bourdeaux, and deprived the city of all its municipal rites and privileges. A conduct ſo oppoſite, produced ſentiments equally diſſimilar in reſpect to the two commanders; and from this æra the family of Guiſe began to date that popularity, which in the ſequel they carried to ſo prodigious and dangerous a length againſt the crown itſelf.

The court meanwhile was immerſed in carouſals and feſtivities. A gallant and
martial

martial prince, who delighted in exertions of prowefs and dexterity, was naturally followed in thofe diverfions by his nobility. Diana de Poitiers, created duchefs of Valentinois, prefided at thefe entertainments, defigned in her honour; and the queen, tho' young and beautiful, tho' of uncommon capacity, and endowed with diffimulation, and manners the moft temporifing, yet acted only an inferior and fubfervient part. She had however the fatisfaction of being crowned at St. Denis; and of making afterwards a triumphal entry with her hufband into the capital: but thefe were only pageantries of ftate; and Henry, who never admitted her to a participation of his authority, feems to have been aware, that her character and genius were more calculated to embroil, than adminifter any remedy to the affairs of government.

By a tranfition wondrous and inexplicable, if any thing in human nature can be efteemed fo, thefe tournaments and entertainments

tainments were immediately fucceeded by exhibitions of a very different nature, but not lefs frequented. — Miftaken piety, a principle the moft pernicious, and ever including a favage and intemperate zeal which delights in blood, was fubftituted in the place of gallantry and pleafure. A number of profelytes to the doctrines of Luther and Calvin were burnt, as an example to their companions. The king and his courtiers were prefent at thefe inhuman facrifices, which were performed with a refinement of mercilefs cruelty, and varied in many fpecies: but it is faid he was fo affected by the dreadful cries of one of his valets de chambre, at whofe execution he attended, that he quitted the place, overcome with horror; and, during his whole remaining life, fo ftrongly were the torments imprinted on his imagination, that he trembled at the recollection, and was feized with remorfe of the moft poignant nature.

 Margaret of Valois, queen of Navarre, died

died nearly about this time, at the caftle of Odos in Bigorre. She had never recovered the affecting news of her beloved brother's death. If Francis the firft was the greateft monarch of his age, Margaret was indifputably the moft accomplifhed princefs. Devoted to the love of letters, fhe encouraged and patronized their authors; from whom fhe received the flattering epithets of, " the Tenth Mufe," and " the Fourth Grace." Herfelf an author, fhe has left us proofs the moft inconteftible of her elegant genius, her wit, and negligent ftyle, full of beauty. Sufpected of Hugonotifm, fhe was fufpected of gallantry likewife; and perhaps might have been equally fenfible in turn to thofe grand movements of elevated minds, devotion and love. Her Tales, fcarce inferior to thofe of Boccacio, feem to confirm this fentiment; and tho' they ever inculcate and commend the virtues of chaftity and female fidelity, yet contain in certain parts an animation, and warmth of colouring, which give room to fuppofe the writer of them fully fenfible to the delights of the paffion fhe cenfured and condemned *.

Boulogne,

* Bonnivet, prefuming on his perfonal attractions, concealed himfelf under her bed, and attempted to violate her honour. She repulfed him, tore off the fkin from his face with her nails, and afterwards complained to the king her brother of this daring attempt; but he only laughed at it. She has related this adventure, fomewhat enigmatically, among her Tales.— Tho' fometimes fo devout as to compofe hymns, yet fhe was certainly an "Efprit fort;" fince fhe had great doubts concerning the immortality of the foul. Brantome has preferved a very curious ftory relative to the death of one of her maids of honour, at which fhe was prefent. The queen was much attached to her, and could not be induced by any entreaties to quit her bed-fide, when expiring. On the contrary, fhe continued to fix her eyes on the dying perfon with uncommon eagernefs and perfeverance, till fhe had breathed her laft. The ladies of her court expreffed to her majefty their aftonifhment and furprife at this conduct; and requefted to know, what fatisfaction fhe could derive from fo clofe an infpection of the agonies of death? Her anfwer marked a moft daring and inquifitive mind. She faid, "that having often heard

"tho

Boulogne, long besieged, was at length surrendered to France, from the weakness and

"the most learned doctors and ecclesiastics assert, that
"on the extinction of the body, the immortal part
"was set at liberty, and unloosed; she could not
"restrain her anxious curiosity to observe if any
"symptoms or indications of such a separation were
"visible or discernible: that none such she had been
"able in any degree to discover; and that, if she was
"not happily very firm in her faith and adherence to
"the catholic religion, she should not know what to
"think of this pretended departure of the soul."

Francis the first took a pleasure in publicly declaring, that to her tenderness, care, and attentions, he was indebted for his life, during the severe illness he underwent in his confinement at Madrid. She had the boldness and spirit to reproach the emperor and his council, in terms the most animated, for their unmanly and cruel treatment of the king. It is said, that Charles was so much irritated by these reprehensions, which he was conscious he merited, that he had intended to seize on her person, and detain her prisoner, if she had outstayed the time granted her to remain in the Spanish dominions. Margaret received intimation of this design; and, without being in the least dismayed, mounted on horseback, crossed the provinces between Madrid and France, and arrived on the

frontier

and diffentions common to a minority; Edward the fixth, king of England, being in very early youth, and his uncle the protector's authority precarious and ill eftablifhed.—The houfe of Guife, firmly united with Diana duchefs of Valentinois, continued to aggrandife itfelf, and gained every year fome new eftablifhment. The genius and great qualities of the duke and cardinal, widely oppofite, but equally pre-

frontier a very few hours before the expiration of her fafe-conduct.

She was feized, fays Brantome, with a catarrh, of which fhe died, while fhe was intently gazing on a comet, fuppofed to predict pope Paul the third's exit. Her illnefs lafted eight days. She feems to have had the fame conftitutional dread and terror of death, which characterifed her mother Louifa. The ladies who attended her announcing to her, when in extremity, that fhe muft prepare herfelf for her end, and fix her thoughts on the joys of a celeftial ftate; "Tout " cela eft vrai," replied the expiring queen; "mais " nous demeurons fi long temps en terre avant que " venir la."—She was above two years older than Francis the firft; and fifty-eight at the time of her deceafe.

eminent

eminent and diftinguifhed, eclipfed all other merit: even the conftable, tho' fuperior to any rival in the royal favour, and poffeffing unlimited influence, yet could not regard unmoved the rapid progrefs they made in univerfal admiration, and beheld with jealoufy thefe new competitors for fame and glory.

Italy, deftined during more than half a century to be the principal fcene of war, again exhibited indications of approaching hoftilities. The grandfons of the late pontiff Paul the third, againft whom Julius the third, newly elected, had taken up arms, and endeavoured to difpoffefs them of the duchy of Parma; claimed the protection of Henry, who gladly afforded it to them. He was charmed to find an occafion for again interfering in the affairs beyond the Alps, and of confequence renewing his attempts on the Milanefe, fo long and fo unfortunately contefted by the French. Briffac was fent into Piedmont, and inftructed to affift the duke of
Parma,

Parma, tho' without any open denunciation againſt the emperor. Julius, after an ineffectual attempt to induce the king to reſign his allies, made as unſuccefsful an effort upon the city, the ſiege of which his general was obliged to raiſe.

Charles, though he had ſcarce paſſed his fiftieth year, was already oppreſſed with all the maladies and infirmities of age. Solyman, his great and conſtant antagoniſt, menaced the Hungarian dominions. He had alarmed all the princes of the empire, by his impriſonment of the landgrave of Heſſe, and his open infringement of the Germanic rights and liberties. Even his brother Ferdinand was juſtly irritated, by his endeavours to compel him to reſign the ſucceſſion of the Imperial crown to Philip prince of Spain, his ſon.—Theſe united conſiderations induced Henry no longer to diſſemble, or delay a rupture with him. Briſſac began the campaign in Piedmont, while Anthony duke of Vendome entered Artois

and

and Hainault. The king ſtrengthened himſelf by a ſecret alliance with Maurice duke of Saxony, head of the proteſtant league; whom he promiſed to aſſiſt with troops and money againſt Charles, who evidently aimed at deſpotiſm.

The effects of this confederacy were ſoon viſible, in the extraordinary and rapid march of Maurice; who had nearly taken the emperor priſoner in Inſpruck, while he amuſed him with propoſals of peace. Charles, terrified, amazed, and on the brink of a ſhameful captivity, fled in a litter by torch-light over the mountains, meanly accompanied; and ſcarce imagined himſelf in ſecurity at Villach in Carinthia, upon the frontier of the Venetian territories. Henry, improving this favourable juncture, marched in perſon into Lorrain; and having firſt poſſeſſed himſelf of the young duke's perſon, ſeized on the cities of Metz, Toul, and Verdun, which, as depending of the empire, were unapprehenſive of, and unprepared for

ſuch

such an attack. These important acquisitions have remained unalterably to France.

Previous to his departure, he vested the regency in the queen, though he at the same time almost associated with her Bertrandi, keeper of the seals, and implicitly devoted to the duchess of Valentinois. Catherine, during the short time in which the administration was entrusted to her, was not guilty of any act injurious to her own character, or the interests of state. That complicated and intriguing genius, that perplexed and pernicious policy, those flattering but ruinous artifices, which so eminently marked her under the reigns of her three children, were as yet unexerted, or unobserved. Accommodating, and mistress of her feelings, she bent beneath madame de Valentinois's superior power; and, so far from making any efforts to diminish or invalidate it, professed for her the most strict and disinterested friendship.

Maurice's

Maurice's fuccefs and mafterly conduct foon reduced the emperor to a neceffity of complying with his offers of peace: and a treaty was figned, which for ever guaranteed and fecured the independence of the German princes, ecclefiaftical and civil. Charles haftened, and gladly accepted thefe overtures, from the defire of revenge on the king of France. The infult and indignity offered him, in the full zenith of his profperity, by the capture of three great cities under the Imperial protection, ftung him with the acuteft fenfations; and, liftening only to his anger, he levied a prodigious army, in the refolution of laying immediate fiege to Metz. The feafon was already far advanced, and it was on the eighteenth day of October when he commenced his attack of it. As the place was however of vaft circuit, and furrounded with fortifications weak and ruinous, he would probably have rendered himfelf mafter of it, if the uncommon exertion of military
fkill

ſkill and virtue in the duke of Guiſe had not fruſtrated his efforts. This great prince, endowed with every talent of a courtier and a warrior, had thrown himſelf into it; and withſtood the emperor's aſſaults with undiſmayed intrepidity, and unſhaken perſeverance. Winter, accompanied with ſnows and the rigours of cold, aided his valour, and conduced to deſtroy the Imperial forces. On the firſt of January Charles diſlodged, after having loſt thirty thouſand ſoldiers, and began his retreat—if ſuch it could be denominated. That acroſs the Alps, after the unfortunate campaign of Provence, was infinitely leſs difaſtrous and miferable than the preſent: and the duke of Guiſe's humanity and care towards the numbers of unhappy wretches who fell into his hands, from the incapacity of accompanying their commander in his flight, ſhone as conſpicuouſly as his courage had done during the ſiege, and rendered his fame immortal.

In

KINGS OF FRANCE, &c.

In Piedmont the war was feebly supported between Briffac and Ferdinand de Gonzague: Solyman, the firm ally of Henry, as he had been of Francis, aided him with his fleets; and by intrigue he gained poffeffion of Sienna; a place which, had it been preferved, would have aided and facilitated, in the greateft degree, any attempts on the Milanefe, or the kingdom of Naples.

The fpring faw the emperor again in the field. Animated with fhame, and anxious to repair his paft defeats, he re-entered France. Terouenne, which refifted his attacks, firft felt the weight of his vengeance. He took, and utterly demolifhed it: Francis de Montmorenci, the conftable's eldeft fon, who had gallantly defended it, remained a prifoner. Emanuel Philibert, the young duke of Savoy, commanded Charles's forces, and began already to difplay that heroifm and martial capacity, which afterwards fo eminently diftinguifhed him. He befieged Hefdin,

Hesdin, which capitulated; but while the articles were under agitation, a grenade thrown by a priest into the town, set fire to a mine, under the ruins of which, Horace Farnese, duke of Castro, grandson to Paul the third, and who had married Diana *, the king's natural daughter, was destroyed with fifty others.—On the other hand, the constable, to whom Henry had committed all his army, performed scarce any exploits worthy an enumeration; and his illness, which followed, put an end to the campaign, and carried his troops into winter quarters.

The death of young Edward, king of England, interrupted the harmony between the

* She was one of the most amiable, accomplished, and beautiful princesses who have appeared in France. Her mother's name was Philippa Duc, of Montcaillier in Piedmont. She was infinitely dear to Henry her father, and not less so to the three succeeding kings her brothers. When left a widow by the duke of Castro's death, she was only fourteen years old. Her name occurs frequently in the narration of Henry the third's life and reign.

two

two crowns. Mary, who succeeded, in opposition equally to the wishes of her people, and of Henry, espoused Philip, the emperor's son. This union, as it encreased the influence and power of Charles's house, was little calculated to diminish the king of France's jealousy, or accelerate a peace. On the contrary, both sides prepared anew for war. The emperor, though disabled by the gout, which had contracted the sinews of one of his legs, and rendered him incapable of using an arm, appeared once more in the field. Henry, who had ever studiously sought the occasion of combating in person his great antagonist, endeavoured to provoke him to a general engagement. He ravaged Hainault, Brabant, and the Cambresis; demolished Mariemont, a palace of pleasure belonging to Mary queen of Hungary, and governess of the Low Countries; and razed the magnificent castle of Bins, which she had lately erected.—Charles marched to the relief of Renty, befieged by the French; and a rude fkirmifh enfued, in which the Imperial forces were obliged to retreat, after a confiderable lofs of men and artillery. The place refifted notwithftanding; and the king, leaving part of his army to the duke of Vendome, difmiffed the remainder, and returned to Paris. Some inconfiderable conquefts which Charles effected, terminated his military exploits, and put an end to all his campaigns.

In Italy, Sienna was loft, after a long and obftinate defence againft the Spaniards; but Briffac maintained the national honour in Piedmont, though ill fupported by the court, and oppofed by the duke of Alva, who vainly and impotently menaced to drive him over the mountains. This gallant commander would even have relieved Sienna, and forced the enemy to raife the fiege, if the oppofition of Montmorenci and the Guifes, jealous of his glory, had not fruftrated his intentions. Mary, Queen of England, attempted to mediate an accommodation

commodation between the contending princes, and a congress was held in a splendid tent near Calais for that purpose; but it produced no beneficial consequences.

The death of Henry d'Albret, king of Navarre, who expired at Hagetmau in Bearn, left his crown and little dominions exposed to the seizure of the French monarch; but the diligence of Anthony duke of Vendome, who had married Jane, heiress to the kingdom, preserved it entire. The king, who had intended to re-unite this small domain to France, by a donation of other lands to Anthony, was highly offended at his conduct; and refusing the government of Picardy to his brother Louis, prince of Condé, conferred it on Coligny.

The emperor, chagrined and mortified at the decline of his lustre, and the successes of Henry; oppressed with diseases, and perhaps tinctured with some of his mother's

mother's * more deplorable and remediless
diforders; determined to refign all his vaft
poffeffions to Philip his fon. He executed
this extraordinary renunciation at Bruſ-
fels, with the referve of the imperial dignity, which he retained a year longer.

The profufion and magnificence of the
court, fuperadded to the wars fuftained
againſt enemies fo powerful, rendered it
neceffary to encreafe the revenues, by additional taxes burdenfome and oppreffive
to the people. Madame de Valentinois

---

* This miferable princefs only finifhed her life fix months before the emperor's abdication. She furvived her hufband, the archduke Philip, forty-nine years, and was above feventy at her own deceafe. Her attachment to him, and his untimely death, chiefly contributed to deprive her of her intellects. She was fhut up in the caftle of Tordefillas, almoft abandoned, fleeping upon ftraw, which fhe fometimes wanted. Her only recreation was to fight with cats, and to crawl up the tapeftry with which her aparments were hung. Such was the lamentable deftiny of Ferdinand and Ifabella's daughter; of the mother of two emperors, and four queens!

was chiefly accufed as the fource of thefe exactions. So far was her influence from any decline, that every year confirmed and extended it. Henry, flexible and eafily led by thofe he loved, only acted through his miftrefs.—She erected the fuperb palace of Anet*, to which the two lovers frequently retired, and which was the chief fcene of their amorous pleafures. Unable to account for fo wondrous and unexampled an attachment, in perfons of fuch unequal ages, the nation attributed it to

* Anet yet exhibits the remains of fplendor and elegance. It is fituated near Dreux, in the Ifle of France. The emblems and devices of the duchefs of Valentinois are vifible in every part of the building. Voltaire has immortalifed it, in thefe beautiful lines of the ninth canto of his Henriade. Love is defcribed as on his way to the plain of Ivry.

"Il voit les murs d'Anet batis aux bords de l'Eure
"Lui-meme en ordonna la fuperbe ftructure;
"Par fes adroites Mains, avec art enlacés,
"Les Chiffres de Diane y font encore tracés;
"Sur fa tombe, en paffant, les plaifirs et les graces
"Repandirent les fleurs qui naiffoient fur leurs
"traces."

forcery,

sorcery, and supernatural causes. It was reported that the duchess wore magical rings, which equally prevented the decay and diminution of her own beauty, or of the monarch's passion.—Catherine of Medicis supported and confirmed this absurd assertion, which soothed her vanity, by accounting for her rival's triumph *.

The

* Monsieur de Thou, though so judicious and able an historian, was not superior to this weakness, characteristic of the age in which he lived; and very gravely mentions as a fact, the magic powers of which Diana availed herself, to perpetuate and support her ascendancy over Henry.——Brantome knew her personally, and has given a minute description of her beauty, in its most advanced period. The passage is too curious and extraordinary to pass over.

" I saw that lady," says he, " only six months be-
" fore she died. She was so lovely at that time, that
" the most insensible person could not have regarded
" her without emotion. She was then on her reco-
" very from a very severe indisposition, consequent to
" a fracture of her leg, which she had broke by a fall
" from her horse, in riding through the streets of Or-
" leans. Yet neither the accident, nor the intense
" pain

The death of pope Julius the third, and the election of Paul the fourth to the pontifical chair, gave another face to the affairs of Italy.—The new pontiff, though more than eighty years of age, and of manners the moſt auſtere, no ſooner attained his new dignity, than aſſuming a conduct the reverſe of that which he had hitherto held, he joined a luxury and pomp unexampled, to projects of the moſt irregular ambition. Irritated by his nephews againſt the emperor, for ſome pretended infractions of which his generals had been guilty, and inflamed with im-

" pain ſhe underwent from it, had in any degree dimi-
" niſhed her charms."

Though Brantome does not abſolutely account for this unparalleled beauty, by any magic influence, yet he endeavours to explain the cauſe of it, by ſomewhat ſimilar means.—" Mais, on dit bien," adds he, " que tous les matins elle uſoit de quelques bouillons " compoſez d'or potable, et autres drogues que je ne " ſçai pas."—At the period of life when he ſpeaks of the duchefs in theſe terms, ſhe was full ſixty-five years old.

potent

potent refentment, he demanded the protection of France, offered the inveftiture of Naples to the king, and endeavoured to negotiate a ftrict alliance for their mutual advantage. — The wifeft and moft difinterefted of the council were averfe to thefe dangerous and chimerical propofitions. They forefaw only difgrace and ruin, in the renewal of the antiquated and remote pretenfions on the crown of Naples; they knew no confidence ought to be repofed on the honour or engagements of Italian politicians, of a man finking under the weight of extreme old age, and actuated by two perfidious and violent nephews. They confidered the ftate of the kingdom, exhaufted by her long and inceffant wars with the emperor, and beholding future ones in profpect againft Philip his fon. They recalled the numerous and ever unfortunate attempts under Louis the twelfth, and Francis the firft, upon the Neapolitan dominions.—Thefe confiderations fo truly weighty,

weighty, ought to have prevented any union or connection with the court of Rome; but the subserviency of all the cabinet to the duke of Guise and his brother, precluded so salutary an advice from Henry's ear. The cardinal of Lorrain, eloquent, impetuous, and vain, embraced the papal overtures with his accustomed enthusiasm, in the intention of placing the duke at the head of the armies destined against Italy. He was immediately dispatched in person to ratify and conclude the treaty; but during his absence, by the intervention of the queen of England, a truce was agreed on for five years between the emperor and France.

To rescind and violate this suspension of hostilities, the cardinal Caraffa was sent, on the part of his uncle the pope, to Paris, with a superb train. He saluted the king at Fontainbleau, presented his majesty a hat and sword, blessed by the sovereign pontiff, and made a magnificent entry into the capital. Intriguing and
artful,

artful, he moved every spring, and availed himself of every means. Catherine and Diana were both rendered subservient to his views. Flattery, presents, vanity, ambition, were by turns exerted or extended to gain their suffrages. Henry, irresolute, unwilling, and after long hesitation, in contradiction to the dictates of his own judgment, suffering himself to be borne away by the torrent, consented to the league.

Francis duke of Guise, nominated to the supreme command, passed the mountains, carrying with him the flower of the nobility, whom the splendor of his character, illustrious for courtesy, courage, and liberality, allured to follow him. None of the Italian powers could be induced to afford him assistance. The pope received him with every mark of external satisfaction, and celebrated his arrival by public festivities and honours; but neither the pecuniary or military aids he had promised, were ready. The duke of Alva, with an army, ravaged the territories of the Church; and the French commander, after an unfuccefsful attempt upon the frontier of Naples, was neceffitated to return for the protection of his allies.—No progrefs was made, no conquefts atchieved; and every thing feemed to portend a termination inglorious and ignominious to his arms, when an event equally difaftrous and unexpected to the kingdom, recalled him from this critical fituation, and extricated him from fo perilous a condition.

Charles, who for near half a century had fpread terror through Europe, no longer acted upon the great political theatre: retired to the monaftery of St. Juftus in Eftremadoura, he was forgotten while yet alive.—Philip, lefs courageous, but not lefs ambitious, affifted by the queen of England, and defirous on his acceffion to imprefs the European princes with ideas of his extenfive power, affembled a prodigious army; but equally
                              deficient

deficient in the bravery and conduct necessary to command it, he entrusted that important commission to the young duke of Savoy. The new general, after a number of feints, attacked the town of St. Quentin in Picardy. Coligny had thrown himself into it, and his obstinate valour served as a rampart to the place, otherwise ill calculated for defence. The constable Montmorenci, his uncle, advanced at the head of his troops, with intent to succour it; but with infinite difficulty did d'Andelot, brother to Coligny, find means to enter with five hundred soldiers. This being effected, he would have retired at noon-day, and in sight of the enemy, superior in numbers, and particularly in cavalry. The duke, conscious of the temerity of the attempt, and seizing instantly the occasion, charged the constable furiously, before he had time to issue the necessary orders, or draw up his forces. The horse were routed, and thrown into confusion; but the infantry

fantry stood firm, and were almost all cut to pieces. Montmorenci himself, with a number of inferior commanders, remained a captive.—Philip, who had not in any degree conduced to this great victory, prevented the decisive effects it might have produced, by his jealousy of the duke of Savoy. Instead of marching without delay to the capital, which was already covered with consternation, and ready to be left desart at his approach, he compelled his general to continue the siege of St. Quentin; which Coligny yet defended some days, and in which he was at length taken prisoner.

Henry meanwhile, in this critical emergency, neglected no measures for the safety of his dominions. Levies of Germans and Switzers were made with all possible expedition; Paris was fortified towards Picardy; the duke of Guise recalled to the defence of France; and even the most pressing solicitations made to Solyman for succour, against the Spanish monarch.

These

Thefe vigorous efforts were attended with a proportionate fuccefs. Re-animated by their prince's firmnefs and intrepidity, and recovering from the firft impreffions of difmay, the Parifians gave the moft diftinguifhed proofs of their loyalty and liberality. The duke of Guife's arrival, the luftre of his name, and reliance upon his great abilities, completed the general tranquillity.—Philip, during the remainder of the campaign, had performed no atchievements, made no acquifitions proportionate to the importance of the battle he had gained. The capture of Ham, Catelet, and Noyon were feeble advantages, and unattended with any decifive confequences.

On the contrary, the duke of Guife, though amid the extreme rigours of winter, loft not a moment to fuccour the drooping genius of his country. After having been declared lieutenant-general within and without the kingdom, he undertook the fiege of Calais, deemed almoft impregnable, and made himfelf mafter of that city,

fo

so long held by the English, in eight days, tho' it had cost Edward the third above a year's blockade. This signal success was followed by the capture of Thionville; but the marechal de Termes, altho' an able and experienced commander, was routed near Gravelines by the young Count d'Egmont; and he himself fell into the enemy's hands.

So astonishing a reverse of fortune served only to heighten and add additional splendor to the reputation of the defender of Metz and conqueror of Calais. He alone, amid the calamities of the state, could command the events of war, and uniformly attach victory to him. On him alone the public confidence rested, as the protecting guardian of France. By a combination of events uniting to the aggrandisement of the house of Guise, their power was still farther confirmed and extended at this juncture, from an alliance which approached them even to the crown.—Francis the dauphin, enamoured of the young queen of Scotland, who had been fent, after her father's death, to the court of Henry for an afylum, obtained the king's confent to his efpoufals.—Mary, fo renowned for her beauty, her talents, and her misfortunes, was at this time in her fixteenth year. Her charms, not yet fully expanded, are yet defcribed by all the French hiftorians, as fo touching and irrefiftible, that a prince of fenfibility, however languid, could not fail to pay homage to them.—Their nuptials were folemnifed with unufual luftre at the church of " Notre Dame," and confummated the fame day, at the " Palais," amid the greateft feftivities.—A triumphal entry into the city fucceeded.—The dauphin was on horfeback, the young bride in a magnificent litter. They affumed the titles of king and queen of England and Scotland, after the death of Mary, which took place the fame year. The court was immerfed in all the gallant entertainments and diverfions natural at fuch a time; and the

duke

duke of Guife, together with the cardinal of Lorrain, found themfelves at the zenith of glory and authority.

Two vaft armies, commanded by their refpective monarchs in perfon, menaced each other on the approach of fpring. Henry and Philip feemed to be on the verge of a decifive engagement; but mutual dread reftrained them, and peace, long delayed, at length was concluded. The conftable, weary of his confinement, anxious for the prefervation of his favour, jealous of the Guifes, and dreading left abfence fhould efface and obliterate that attachment the king had borne him, requefted and obtained permiffion to go to him in perfon, in the defign of procuring a general pacification. He was received with teftimonies of the warmeft affection, and moft unabated friendfhip, by his mafter; who carried his condefcenfion and fondnefs to fo great a pitch, as to make him lie in his own bed. It was determined to put an end to the war, at whatever price, or by whatever sacrifices. After several conferences at Cercamp, the preliminaries were finally adjusted, and signed at Cateau in Cambresis.—All the Italian acquisitions, gained in the late and present reign, in Piedmont, Tuscany, and Corsica, were ceded, to procure the restitution of three inconsiderable towns in Picardy.—Calais, Metz, Toul, and Verdun remained to France.—The princess Margaret, sister to the king, was affianced to the duke of Savoy; and Isabella, his eldest daughter, taken from Don Carlos, Philip's son, for whom she was first designed, and given to Philip himself, become a widower by the queen of England's death.

These terms, humiliating and ignominious to France, were attributed to the constable; who from interested motives, and the desire of terminating his captivity, had counselled the king to accept them. The Guises loudly decried and arraigned them, as unworthy and unbecoming the national honour, and depriving the kingdom

dom in a moment of the conquests of near thirty years; but Henry was immoveable, and adhered to his refolution.

During the reign of Francis the firft, and more peculiarly fo fince his deceafe, the reformed religion had made a moft alarming and univerfal progrefs. All ranks of people had imbibed the new doctrines; and perfecution unhappily being fuperadded, haftened and promoted their influence. D'Andelot, nephew to the conftable, and brother to Coligny, was juftly fufpected, and even accufed of being a profelyte to thefe opinions. Henry, defirous to be fatisfied of the truth or falfhood of the imputation, queftioned him perfonally, what he thought of the Mafs; and d'Andelot, with imprudent zeal, made him fo bold and undifguifed a reply, that, irritated to a pitch of frantic indignation, he was about to have put him to death with his own hand.—It required all his uncle's intereft to procure his pardon, and reftitution to his poft of colonel in the infantry,

infantry. The moſt ſevere penalties were denounced againſt the profeſſors of Calviniſm; and ſeveral members of the parliament, having preſumed to declare againſt the rigour of the puniſhments enacted and executed on them, the king himſelf went in perſon, and ordered five of them to be arreſted and carried to the Baſtile immediately, who had avowed that ſentiment in his preſence. Orders were iſſued for their prompt and rigorous proſecution.

With the return of tranquillity and peace, every ſpecies of luxurious diſſipation revived. Henry's court, the moſt effeminate, debauched, and poliſhed in Europe, was rendered unuſually ſplendid by the different entertainments exhibited on occaſion of the marriage of Iſabella to Philip. It was celebrated by proxy at Paris. Tournaments and carouſals added a martial magnificence to the other amuſements of a gentler nature. The duke of Savoy arriving, accompanied by the duke of Brunſwic, the prince of Orange,

Orange, and a hundred gentlemen, was received with every demonſtration of reſpect and attention by Henry; who met and embraced him at the foot of the great ſtair-caſe of the Louvre. This incident redoubled the feſtivities. Only three days after, they were interrupted by the tragical cataſtrophe of the king's death.

The liſts extended from the palace of the Tournelles to the Baſtile, acroſs the ſtreet St. Antoine. Henry himſelf had broken ſeveral lances with different lords of the court, in all of which he had ſhewn unuſual vigour and addreſs. On that day he wore the colours of his miſtreſs, the duchefs of Valentinois, in token of his homage, and in compliance with the laws of chivalry, where gallantry was ever mingled. Thoſe colours were black and white, in alluſion to her ſtate of widowhood.—Towards the cloſe of the evening, and previous to the concluſion of the tournament, he was ſeized with the inclination of trying his prowefs againſt the

count

count de Montgomeri, captain in his guards. He was fon to that feigneur de Lorges, who had wounded Francis the firſt fo dangerouſly on the head at Romorentin in Berri; and was diſtinguiſhed for his fuperiority in thefe combats above any nobleman of the kingdom.—Catherine of Medicis, as if by a fecret prefage of the event, befought him not to re-enter the liſts; Henry refifted her folicitations; adding, that he would break one more lance in her honour. Montgomeri himfelf accepted the defiance with extreme reluctance, and endeavoured by every argument and entreaty to prevail on his fovereign to excufe him; but in vain. Henry commanded him to obey. He even fought with his vizor raifed. The fhock was rude on both fides; but the count's lance breaking againſt the king's helmet, he attacked him with the ſtump, which remained in his hand. It entered under the eyebrow of his right eye. The blow was fo violent, as to tumble

tumble him to the ground, and to deprive him inftantly both of his fpeech and underftanding. He never more recovered them, though he furvived the accident near eleven days.—The queen ordered him to be carried immediately to the Tournelles: every medical affiftance was procured, and the divine mercy implored by proceffions and public prayers:—but the wound was beyond a cure; and he at length expired, having only paffed his fortieth year four months.

Confternation and affright, mingled with intrigue and artifice, divided the court: and the number of contending factions, headed by chiefs of the higheft capacity, whom the late king's vigour had reftrained within fubjection, now declared their various pretenfions without difguife.—The duke of Savoy, finding his life defpaired of, folicited fo preffingly the accomplifhment of his matriage with the princefs Margaret, that it was celebrated at " Notre-Dame," without any pomp, and

and in the greateſt privacy.—The duchefs of Valentinois received an order from the queen to retire to her own hotel, and not to prefume to enter the chamber of the dying king. She obeyed.—Catherine followed this mandate by a fecond, enjoining her to deliver up the jewels of the crown, and other rich effects then in her poſſeſſion. She demanded, if Henry was dead; the meſſenger replied, that he yet breathed; but could not poſſibly remain long alive. "Know," faid Diana, with undaunted intrepidity, "that fo "long as he fhall retain the leaſt appear- "ance of life, I neither fear my enemies, "however powerful, nor will fhew any "deference to their menaces or com- "mands. Carry this anfwer to the "queen."

If Henry was not a great, he was an amiable and accompliſhed prince. Generous to his domeſtics, bounteous to his followers, he was adored by his courtiers and attendants. His converfation was

amufive

amufive and lively; his manner of expreffion eloquent, flowing, and graceful. An affectionate father, a polite and decent hufband, a warm and animated friend, he was, in all the walks of private life, peculiarly an object of refpect and attachment. Neither deftitute of capacity or firmnefs, though governed by his miftrefs, and fubfervient to favourites, he could exert himfelf on important occafions, and enforce obedience. Fond of polite letters, as from hereditary right, he encouraged them in his court, where they made a rapid progrefs. In the prime of life, and with fuch qualities, his death muft at any time have been confidered as a lofs to his kingdom;—but in the critical juncture when he expired, it was a calamity of the moft dreadful nature, replete with future miferies, with maffacres, crimes, and civil difcord. He only could reprefs the daring fpirit and intemperate zeal of the new religions: he only could reftrain the intriguing genius of Catherine, and

fet

fet bounds to the wild ambition of the princes of the houfe of Lorrain. His untimely end, and the fucceeding circumftances of his fons' reigns, unveiled and gave a loofe to every fource of public evil and diftrefs.

By the queen he left a numerous iffue; four fons and three daughters. They will be all mentioned frequently hereafter. He never had any children by madame de Valentinois;—but befides Diana, married to the duke of Caftro, of whom I have already fpoken, he left a fon by a Scotch lady *, named Henry; who

* Her name is faid to have been Fleming; and fhe was in the fervice of Mary queen of Scotland, whom fhe had accompanied from her own country into France: yet others of the cotemporary writers call her " Mademoifelle d'Amilton ;" and pretend, that fhe was related to Mary by blood. They add, that motives of policy and intrigue gave rife to the connection between this lady and the king.—The Guifes, jealous of the defpotic afcendant which Diana de Poitiers had obtained and preferved over him, determined

who was grand prior of France, governor of Provence, and admiral of the Levant feas.

We termined to detach him from her; as they found she no longer treated them with her accuftomed confidence; and that Montmorenci had fupplanted them in her affections.—To this end, they artfully praifed " Mademoifelle d'Amilton," and extolled her to Henry with extravagant eulogiums. He faw and loved her. She did not fcruple to gratify his paffion; but their intimacy was concealed, even after fhe had borne a fon, with the extremeft care, to prevent its becoming known to the duchefs of Valentinois.— Henry d'Angouleme, her fon, was a generous, brave, and accomplifhed prince, though unhappily led, by the prejudices and madnefs of the times, to be eminently active in the dreadful night of St. Bartholomew.—His death was tragical and fingular. It happened at Aix in Provence. Philip Altoviti, baron de Caftelane, was his mortal enemy; Henry entered his houfe, and, after having reproached him with his many acts of malignant hatred towards him, paffed his fword through his body. Altoviti expiring, had yet fufficient force to fnatch a poniard from the head of the bed on which he fell, with which he ftabbed Henry in the belly. He did not apprehend his wound to be mortal; but the friar who confeffed him, an-

nouncing

We are now about to enter on a melancholy period of the French hiftory. Wars of religion, more fanguinary, more cruel, more obftinate and ruinous, than thofe of Henry the fifth and Edward the third, rife in awful fucceffion under the three laft princes of the race of Valois. The bright days of Francis and Henry, the noble and animating contefts with Charles and Philip, are fucceeded by inteftine confufion, by the ftandard of rebellion and revolt. The kingdom, inundated with foreign auxiliaries, torn by her own children, drenched in noble blood, becomes a field of contention and defolation. Catherine, like its evil genius, mingles and embroils all ranks and parties. The fpirit of civil and religious frenzy fwallows up and extinguifhes every fentiment of humanity, patriotifm,

nouncing to him his deftiny, he replied, without emotion, " Il ne faut plus penfer à vivre ? Eh bien, pen-
" fons donc à mourir !"—He died twenty-four hours afterwards.

and even virtue—till at length a ſtranger prince, deſcended from the blood of their ancient kings, appears; and, as if ſent from Heaven to heal the wounds of his bleeding country, reſtores peace, and diffuſes univerſal ſerenity.

CHAPTER

CHAPTER THE NINTH.

State of the kingdom at the death of Henry the second.—Character of the duke of Guife—of the cardinal of Lorrain—of the king of Navarre—of the prince of Condé.—Catherine of Medicis.—Her character—perfon—political conduct.—Difgrace of the duchefs of Valentinois.—Acceffion of Francis the fecond.—Power of the Guifes.—The king's feeble health.—Affaffination of Minard.—Confpiracy of Amboife.—Defeated.—Horrible executions.—The prince of Condé fufpected.—Convocation of Fontainbleau.—The king of Navarre and prince of Condé arrive at court.—They are arrefted.—Trial of the latter.—Francis's illnefs.—Condé condemned.—Intrigues and cabals of Catherine de Medicis.—Death of Francis the fecond.—Circumftances.—Character.—Funerals.—Arrival of Montmorenci.—Releafe of Condé.

PREVIOUS to our entry upon this
short but unhappy reign, which first
gave birth to the wars of Calvinism, and
saw the sword of France unsheathed
against herself; it is requisite to take a
view of the great personages who will
appear upon the scene, and behold the
elements of future calamities yet latent
and concealed, or only faintly unfolding
the fatal principles of destruction with
which they were impregnated. The un-
foreseen and sad catastrophe of Henry
the second's death, awoke these dormant
seeds, which might otherwise have slept
in tranquillity. That superior and coer-
cive power being removed, that had hitherto over-ruled the many jarring and
discordant spirits with which the court
was filled, a tumultuous administration
succeeded, precarious in its basis, uncertain in its duration, and only supported
by an extraordinary exertion of vigilance,
circumspection, and authority.

Amid the confufion incident to the deceafe of the late king, the Guifes had feized upon the perfon of Francis the fecond, the young fovereign. Their alliance by blood to the queen, Mary of Scotland, afforded them a plaufible pretext to juftify their conduct; and the characters of the two brothers, Francis duke of Guife and the cardinal of Lorrain, feemed to render them intitled to the firft pofts of ftate.

The former poffeffed eminently all thofe dazzling qualities which are formed to procure an unlimited afcendancy over mankind. Liberal even to munificence, courteous to condefcenfion in his manners and addrefs, he captivated the multitude. His renown in arms procured him the adoration of the foldiery, and attachment of the braveft captains, who deemed themfelves certain of fuccefs under his aufpices. Naturally moderate, equitable, and averfe to cruelty, he yet zealoufly maintained the ancient religion, and oppofed every innovation. Intrepid in the article of danger,

ger, either perfonal or political, he furveyed it without trouble or difmay, and applied to it the moft prompt and efficacious remedies. Confcious of his own capacities for government, favoured by the peculiar circumftances of the times, and hurried away by his ambition, he gave the reins to this paffion, and fet no limits to his thirft of power.

Talents of an oppofite nature, but no lefs feductive and impofing, characterifed his brother the cardinal. Eloquent, and animated with unbounded zeal in the caufe of the catholic religion, he was venerated by the clergy, as the guardian of the ecclefiaftical immunities and privileges. Inferior to the duke in clemency and tempered courage, he was more enterprizing, prefumptuous, and vain. Elated to arrogance with fuccefs, he funk into pufillanimity and unmanly terror, when oppreffed by adverfe fortune. Violent, irafcible, and vindictive, he could not reftrain or diffemble his feelings. Diffolute, and

fond

fond of pleafure, he gave offence by the libertinifm of his conduct. Greedy of power, rapacious of wealth, facrificing every meaner confideration of tendernefs or affection to the dictates of a ftern and unrelenting policy, he knew no movements, nor purfued any objects, except thofe of elevation and aggrandifement.

Anthony, king of Navarre, firft prince of the blood, was ill calculated to oppofe thefe afpiring and turbulent fpirits. Of a temper gentle, humane, and flexible, nature feemed to have defigned him for times of harmony and tranquillity. Equal to the duke of Guife in perfonal bravery, he was far beneath him in every other point of competition. Politically timid, inconftant, irrefolute, he wanted that firmnefs fo indifpenfable in great emergencies. Fluctuating in endlefs uncertainty between the two religions, he neither could be deemed a Catholic or Hugonot. Voluptuous, and fond of women, he was eafily induced to break his conventions of policy,

licy, in the weakneſs of private attachment.

Far other was his brother the prince of Condé. His perſon little and ungraceful, incloſed a ſoul the moſt heroic. Amorous from complexion, and of an addreſs the moſt perſuaſive, he was beloved by women, and received from them proofs of their affection the moſt unbounded and intoxicating. Of high and determined courage, he was formed to ſhine in camps as much as courts. Indigent in his fortunes almoſt to penury, he had yet the liberality becoming his high birth. Profeſſing with zeal the doctrines of Calvin, but little inclined to the rigorous manners of the Reformation, he made religion the pretext of thoſe wars, which ambition, and hatred to the Guiſes, really produced. Not inferior to the celebrated Charles of Bourbon in the arts of retaining a licentious ſoldiery in ſubjection, nature had intended him for war, and veſted him with all her capacities for the attainment of military glory.

With qualities such as I have described, he formed no unequal antagonist to the duke of Guise; whom he ever considered as his mortal enemy, and boldly opposed on all occasions.

The constable Montmorenci, long accustomed to occupy the first post of state, and too haughty to fill an inferior one, did not at once declare for either faction; but the pressing instances of Henry d'Amville his second son, and his natural aversion to Hugonotism, induced him at length to join the princes of the house of Lorrain.

The marechal de St. André, one of the most accomplished noblemen of the court, brave, polite, and elegant, but immersed in pleasures, and ruined by his debts, ranged himself under the same banner, and devoted himself implicitly to the duke of Guise's service.——On the contrary, Coligni, and d'Andelot his brother, both avowed proselytes to Calvinism, embraced the party of the princes of the blood, and adhered to it invariably.

Catherine

Catherine of Medicis, whom we have so long beheld obscured by the superior influence of the two successive mistresses to Francis and Henry, now first came forward, and rose into importance. Her rank, as mother to the young king, made her friendship eagerly sought by every party. Her talents and capacity rendered her equal to, and capable of the most arduous offices of government. A character too complicated, and containing movements too numerous and intricate for a common description, I scarce dare to attempt this difficult picture.

Endowed by nature with a thousand qualities great and shining, she only wanted virtue to direct them to honourable and salutary ends. Fond of pleasure, of letters, of magnificence, these were yet only inferior movements: ambition predominated, and swallowed up all other passions in her bosom. Born with a force of mind, a calmness and self-possession which might have done honour to the boldest man, nan, fhe feemed to look down as from an eminence on human occurrences. Never alarmed even in circumftances the moft unexpected and diftrefsful, fhe knew how to bend and accommodate herfelf to them. Of confummate diffimulation, her manners, where fhe wifhed to fucceed in any attempt, were ingratiating beyond the powers of female feduction. Sprung from the blood of Cofmo de Medecis, and emulative of the fame which Francis the firft had acquired by his protection of learning, fhe cultivated poetry, and all the humanizing arts, amid the horrors of civil war; and extended her generofity to men of genius, even in the moft exhaufted ftate of the finances.—Expenfive even to prodigality in the entertainments and diverfions fhe exhibited, and covering her defigns under the deceitful mafk of diffipation, fhe planned a maffacre amid the feftivities of a banquet, and careffed with the moft winning blandifhments the victim fhe had deftined to deftruction. Cruel from policy,

licy, not from temper, avaricious from neceffity, profufe from tafte, fhe united in herfelf qualities the moſt difcordant and contradictory.

Her perfon was noble, and correfponded with her dignity: the beauty of her countenance was blended with majefty. She knew how to improve her natural charms by all the magic of drefs, and carried her magnificence on this article to a prodigious length. Expert in every exercife of the body, fhe fhone equally diftinguifhed in the dance, and in the chace. Her attractions were not fugitive and frail, but accompanied her even into age, and hardly quitted her in her moft advanced period of life *.

Thefe

* Her complexion was unufually fine, her eyes large, full of vivacity and fire. She had, when young, a faultlefs fhape; but grew afterwards large and corpulent. Her head was difproportionately big; nor could fhe walk any confiderable diftance, without being fubject to a dizzinefs and fwimming. The extream fymmetry and admirable fhape of her legs,
made

These are only faint and imperfect outlines of a portrait, which must be known by study, not description; and which the events of the three succeeding reigns will afford me continual opportunity to retouch and correct.

While Henry, mortally wounded, lay expiring, Catherine, though externally

made her take a particular pleasure in wearing silk stockings drawn very tight, the use of which were first introduced in her time ; and the desire of shewing them more conspicuously, induced her to change the mode of riding on horseback, which was by resting the feet on a small board, to that of placing one leg upon the pommel of the saddle.—Catherine piqued herself on the address with which she rode; and tho' by her boldness in hunting she once broke a leg, and at another time received so severe a blow on the head, as to be obliged to undergo the trepan, she continued this exercise to her sixtieth year. Her hands and arms excelled any lady's of the court, both as to form and whiteness.—All habits became her, from the refined taste with which she adjusted every ornament to her figure ; and her wardrobe was equally varied and splendid. Her neck and breast were of the most matchless and dazzling white. Brantome speaks of them with enthusiastic praise and pleasure.

agitated

agitated with the deepest sorrow, yet provident of futurity, and foreseeing the natural consequence of her son's accession, hesitated in suspence what measures to embrace. Though she dreaded the capacity, the ambition, the influence of the Guises, yet the constable was more personally and immediately obnoxious to her. He had lately united himself closely with madame de Valentinois; and had likewise started suspicions the most injurious to her honour and fidelity, by asserting, that of all the children which she had brought her husband, not one resembled him. On the contrary, the princes of Lorrain courted her friendship, and promised her the sacrifice of the late king's mistress, as the cement of their common union. This tempting condition, so grateful to a woman's vengeance, determined the queen. Diana, abandoned by the croud of parasites and courtiers, who had surrounded her in Henry's reign, underwent in turn the humiliation of the duchess of Estampes;

tampes; and retired immediately from a theatre, where her prefence was grown hateful, and her power become extinct. She fpent the remainder of her days at Anet: and Catherine, fatisfied with a political victory, and repreffing, from regard to her hufband's memory, any further purfuit, permitted her to retain all the fplendid donations fhe had gained from the bounty of her lover, without diminution *.

The

* It cannot be denied that the queen acted with the higheft magnanimity and clemency on this occafion; fhe might have taken a bloody and exemplary revenge on her hateful rival. The marechal de Tavannes offered to cut off her nofe; but Catherine would not permit or confent to it. The Guifes, though intimately connected with her, and though principally indebted to her for their elevation and favour, yet were fo bafe as to become her open enemies on Henry's death. — The cardinal of Lorrain would have been her bittereft perfecutor, if his brother, the duke of Aumale, who had married her daughter, had not reftrained, and reminded him, " That it would cover " himfelf with infamy, to become the executioner

" of

The young king, Francis the second, who ascended the throne, was only sixteen years and six months old. A weakness both corporal and intellectual, approaching to debility, incapacitated him, even more than his unripe age, for the conduct of state affairs. Merely actuated by his mother, and by the two princes, uncles to the queen consort; he had neither judgment or passions to direct himself, or withstand their advice and suggestions.—When the deputies of the parliament waited on him, to express their devotion and duties, he therefore informed them, that he had thought proper to invest the duke and cardinal with the supreme administration, assigning to the former the

" of his mother-in-law.—The constable would not desert her, from respect to the memory of his benefactor Henry the second, though urged to that purpose.—Diana expressed her gratitude to the queen, by a present of the superb palace of Chaumont, situated in the midst of those lands assigned her for dowry; and received from her in return the castle of Chenonceaux.

military

military department, and the finances to the latter.

The conſtable, who early ſaw this inevitable triumph of his enemies, had advertiſed the king of Navarre, and beſought him to repair immediately to court, and claim the authority to which his high rank and birth eminently entitled him; but Anthony, ſlow, incapable of a bold and deciſive reſolution, and diſtruſtful of Montmorenci's attachment, advanced by ſhort journies, and ſtopt at Vendome. This ill-judged and tardy conduct, gave the Guiſes time to confirm their acquiſition, and ſtrengthen their power. Montmorenci, remanded into a ſecond exile, was ordered to retire to his own houſe. The cardinal of Tournon was recalled, and admitted to an apparent aſſociation in the government. Bertrandi, to whom Diana de Poitiers had cauſed the ſeals to be entruſted, was diſmiſſed; and Olivier, a man renowned for probity and honour, created chancellor.

Meanwhile

Meanwhile Anthony, ſtimulated by his brother the prince of Condé, arrived at length. His reception was cold even to indignity : the lodging aſſigned him was unworthy his quality, and he would have remained deſtitute of any, if the marechal de St. André had not lent him the one he occupied. When preſented to the new king, Francis made him the ſame declaration he had already done to his parliament. His friends ſtill exhorted him to remain unſhaken, and wait the opportunity of regaining his intereſt and credit : but the Guiſes acting on his terrors, by indirect menaces of the king of Spain's reſentment, if he preſumed to controvert the queen mother's or her ſon's choice of miniſters ; and Catherine, on the other hand, alluring him with a promiſe of procuring the reſtitution of his ancient kingdom of Navarre, he ſubmitted. After the ceremony of the coronation, he was ſent to conduct the young queen Iſabella to her huſband, Philip the ſecond.

Confcious of the precarious foundation on which their authority refted, and dreading fome attempt upon it, the new minifters publifhed an edict, forbidding to carry fire-arms, or even any drefs favourable to the concealment of fuch weapons: This order, calculated for their perfonal fafety, and indicative of diftruft and terror, was followed by a fecond, which their intereft dictated. The king declared, that he would permit no perfon to hold two pofts at the fame time. Coligni, who to the high charge of admiral, joined the government of Picardy, refigned chearfully the latter, in the expectation that it would be conferred on the prince of Condé; but Briffac, recalled from his command in Piedmont, was invefted with it. The conftable reluctantly, and after many delays, laid down his office of grand mafter of the houfhold, beftowed on him by his late fovereign's bounty; and the duke of Guife fucceeded to it.

Animated by an intemperate zeal, the minifters

ministers persuaded their weak prince, that he only adhered to his father's maxims and conduct, in commencing a persecution against the Hugonots. Courts of ecclesiastical judicature, armed with inquisitorial powers, were erected, which took cognizance of heresy; they were denominated the " Chambres ardentes," from the severity of the punishments they inflicted. The most rigorous search was made to discover offenders; crimes of the most improbable and flagitious nature imputed to them, in their nocturnal assemblies; and a death accompanied with ignominy, heightened by cruelty, was decreed for their adherence to Calvinism. It was not confined to the capital. The provinces imitated the example; and these unhappy people, forced into opposition, and emboldened by religious despair, began to attempt a defence against their oppressors.

The prodigious number of troops disbanded in consequence of the late peace;

the swarms of military adventurers whom the cession of the Luxembourg and Piedmont left unemployed, added to the sources of intestine commotion, and disclosed to the Calvinists the means of raising forces in case of necessity. The court was crouded with soldiers of fortune, who importunately demanded some recompence for their services. The cardinal of Lorrain, to whom they principally addressed their petitions, unable to satisfy them, and apprehensive of some conspiracy in this multitude, published a rash edict, which commanded every person, who had any favour to ask of the king, instantly to withdraw themselves, on pain of being hung up on a gibbet, which was erected for that purpose in the public square. A treatment so unworthy and unprecedented, irritated extremely all those against whom it was directed, and alienated from him and the duke many brave officers, who were before devotedly attached to the house of Guise.

Francis's

Francis's health meanwhile, debilitated and enfeebled by diftempers, gave alarming tokens of decay. A quartan ague, with which he had been indifpofed during feveral months, totally incapacitated him for any application to bufinefs of ftate. When this diforder left him, his face was covered with puftules, which evinced the malignant nature of his humours. He was therefore carried to Blois, in hopes of benefit from the change of air. The ufual methods practifed to diminifh or abate the acrimony of fcorbutic habits, were tried. A report prevailed, and even was univerfally credited in the environs of Blois, that the blood of infants was procured, to make him a bath. The fame had been afferted of Louis the eleventh, in his laft illnefs, though probably without foundation. From the remedies adminiftered, of whatever kind, he however derived fome temporary benefit and relief.

Meanwhile the feverities againft the

professors of the Reformed religion were redoubled at Paris. Anne du Bourg, one of the five members of the parliament, whom Henry the second had committed to the Baſtile a few weeks before his death, was tried; and continuing pertinaciouſly in his opinions, was capitally condemned. His execution was accelerated by the aſſaſſination of the preſident Minard, one of his judges; to whom he had peculiarly objected, and who had been zealouſly active in the seizure and conviction of the Calviniſts. The authors of this crime were never diſcovered. Robert Stuart, a native of Scotland, and who was afterwards in the battle of St. Denis, where he mortally wounded the conſtable, was suſpected and ſeized. He claimed the young queen's protection, to whom he declared himſelf related by blood. Mary diſowned his alliance, and would extend no mark of favour towards him. Stuart found reſources in his own firmneſs and intrepidity: he underwent

the

the moſt excruciating pains of torture without any confeſſion; and was therefore abſolved and difmiſſed.

Puſhed to reſolutions of the moſt deſperate nature, by the ill-judged tyranny of their perſecutors, and oppoſing the undaunted ſpirit of religious conviction, to the ſuperior power of their enemies, the Calviniſts began ſecretly to unite for their common preſervation. Neither Louis prince of Condé, nor Coligni, though notoriouſly proſelytes to the new opinions, had yet declared themſelves their chieftains. A gentleman of Angoumois, named John de Bary la Renaudie, was commiſſioned, notwithſtanding, by the principal perſons among them, to collect a number under proper leaders, who, by different roads, ſhould meet at Blois; and, having preſented a petition to the king, ſhould ſeize on the perſons of the duke of Guiſe and cardinal of Lorrain, as enemies to the kingdom and public tranquillity. The ſecret, ill kept, was divulged, and

and information sent of the conspirators' intentions, to court, from many quarters. The Guises, warned of the coming storm, took every measure necessary to avert it. Francis was removed from Blois to the castle of Amboise, as more tenable, and capable of defence. He issued letters, commanding the prince of Condé's and admiral's attendance; who obeyed. The duke's title of lieutenant-general of the kingdom was confirmed; bodies of soldiery were stationed on all the surrounding roads; and a company of musqueteers, mounted on horseback, was raised to guard the person of the king.

Notwithstanding these judicious and masterly precautions, the conspirators, in small bands, and marching only during the night, appeared at the gates of Amboise, unexpectedly. The cardinal of Lorrain, terrified at this approach of danger, betrayed the timidity which was natural to him; but his brother the duke, undismayed, and master of himself, instantly ftantly prepared to meet it with courage. His cool difcernment appeared eminently confpicuous in this hour of trial. He affembled the guards, the nobility, and inhabitants. Cautious, and fufpecting the prince of Condé, he gave him the poft of one of the gates to defend; but took care to accompany him with the grand-prior, one of his own brothers, who watched all his movements, and prevented him from lending the moft indirect affiftance.

The Calvinifts were difperfed, taken, or cut in pieces. La Renaudie, with a few affociates, was met in the foreft of Chateau-Renaud by the baron de Pardillan, at the head of two hundred cavalry. He defended himfelf, notwithftanding the difparity of numbers, with a bravery heightened by defpair. His followers being almoft all flain, and no chance remaining either of victory or retreat, he fpurred his horfe up to Pardillan, and thrufting a poniard through his vizor, laid him dead upon the ground. He himfelf fell foon after by a ball from a harquebuffe. When killed, his body was brought to Amboife, and hung during fome hours on a gallows erected upon the bridge.—All the inferior perfons who fell, were treated with the fame ignominy. Their bodies, dragged at the tails of the horfes, were afterwards placed on iron hooks round the walls of the caftle, completely habited, booted, and fpurred.

Some clemency might yet have been fhewn towards the chiefs. Olivier, the chancellor, warmly advifed lenient and conciliating meafures. Even the Guifes hung in fufpence whether to pardon or punifh; when a new, but impotent attempt to furprife the town, gave a loofe to the laft feverity. All who were taken in arms, even though on their return home, were put to death. A number not lefs than twelve hundred expired under the executioner's hands. The ftreets of Amboife ran purple with blood; the Loire was covered with floating carcafes;

and the public fquares were crowded with gibbets, on which hung thefe unhappy wretches, who infected the air with a peftilential fmell.

The principal leaders were laft led out to die. The queen-mother, with her three young fons, and all the principal ladies of the court, beheld this horrid fpectacle from the windows, as a diverfion. Two of them, under the agony of the Queftion, accufed the prince of Condé as their accomplice, though concealed; but the baron de Caftelnau, confronted with them, denied it highly, and in the moment previous to his head being fevered from his body, attefted and confirmed the prince's innocence.

Some fufpicions remaining againft him, notwithftanding thefe favourable depofitions, he demanded permiffion to clear himfelf in full council before the king. Catherine, ever endeavouring to fupport the balance between the grandees, as moft beneficial to her own interefts, granted his
demand.

demand. The prince, with that generous intrepidity which shone in all his actions, vindicated his honour from the treasonable imputations cast upon it; and, after having given the lye to whoever dared to maintain or assert them, offered to engage in single combat, as the most convincing proof of his adversary's falsehood. The cardinal of Lorrain, who clearly saw at whom this defiance was levelled, made a sign to the young monarch to rise without reply; but his brother the duke, concealing his indignation with dissembled friendship, praised with warmth the prince's noble conduct, and offered likewise to maintain his cause against whatever antagonist. Yet in private, he advised to arrest him; but the queen-mother, who foresaw the utter annihilation of her power by such an act, opposed and prevented its execution.

The chancellor died at this time, of grief and horror, excited by the cruel and sanguinary scenes to which he had been a witness.

witnefs. He was fucceeded by Michael de l'Hopital, an able minifter, and devoted to the queen-mother. His advice confirmed her yet more in that temporizing and intricate policy, in that perfidious hypocrify, in thofe arts of divifion and oppofition, which mark her character. She trembled left the Guifes fhould obtain a complete victory over the princes of the blood, and therefore fecretly fupported Coligni and the Hugonots. A convocation was fummoned in this view at Fontainbleau, whither the king was tranfferred. It was held in her own cabinet, Francis being prefent. The admiral advancing, threw himfelf on his knees before his fovereign, and prefented a requeft unfigned, in favour of his own fect; adding, that though no names were affixed to it, yet, whenever his majefty pleafed, it would be inftantly fubfcribed by an hundred and fifty thoufand perfons. The cardinal of Lorrain oppofed it, with that floury, impetuous, and commanding eloquence,

quence, which diſtinguiſhed him. No deciſive reſolution was taken; but the ſtates were ordered to aſſemble, and a national council propoſed, in hopes of finally adjuſting theſe religious differences.

Neither Anthony or Louis were preſent at this conference. They had retired into Guyenne, where they were engaged in concerting meaſures to diſpoſſeſs the Guiſes of their power and offices. The perſon whom they employed as their confidant and meſſenger, named La Sague, was ſeized at Eſtampes, on his return into Gaſcony, charged with a number of letters. The terror of the torture made him confeſs the method of diſcovering their contents. Thoſe of the vidame of Chartres were regarded as peculiarly criminal. He was one of the moſt brave and gallant lords of the court, and had been ſo particularly acceptable to, and favoured by Catherine, as to give riſe to ſuſpicions and accuſations very injurious to her honour,

nour. As he was however now become equally an object of her hatred, she caused him to be carried to the Baſtile. He was transferred some time after to his own house, where he died either of chagrin, or the consequences of his debaucheries *.

Bouchard, chancellor to the king of Navarre, being seized, and actuated by the same timidity as La Sague, accused the prince of Condé with endeavours to

---

* The proteſtant writers, who detested Catherine, have not failed to accuse her of gallantries, among her other crimes. Jurieu particularly names the duke of Nemours, the vidame of Chartres, and the marquis de Mescouet, as her lovers; and declares her to have been criminally intimate with all these. Impartial juſtice muſt, however, acquit her from these imputations. Ambition, not love, was her predominant movement. Her conduct towards mademoiselle de Limeuil, of which I shall have occaſion to ſpeak minutely, was highly oppoſed to any such libertiniſm.—Mezerai, and " Le Laboureur," only blame her love of pleaſures, without any reflections on her honour; which are certainly to be diſtruſted as falſe aſperſions.

seduce

seduce his brother to treasonable practices. Notwithstanding this act of undisguised hostility, they both remained unshaken in their resolution of attending the states at Orleans *. Their friends advised them
to

* Davila, the great directing historian of these times, beautifully lays open the manœuvres of the Guises to draw the brothers into the snare. Louis, says he, conscious that his co-operation in the late conspiracies and commotions might be ascertained from the papers and persons lately seized, peremptorily refused to trust himself in the power of his enemies:—but Anthony, either more innocent, or more credulous; and deeming it impossible, that an Italian woman, and two strangers, would venture to arrest and punish the princes of the blood, inclined to attend the states. The count de Crussol, and the marechal de St. André, were dispatched by the king, to induce them, by dissembled assurances of amity, not to delay their journey. Condé still remained firm in his determination. This being reported, the marechal de Termes was sent into Gascony, and ordered to levy a body of troops, which might invest them in Bearn, where they were unprepared for defence. At the same time, the queen-mother, ever effecting her schemes by dissimulation, prevailed on the cardinal of Bourbon, brother to Anthony and Louis, to add
his

to appear well armed, and numeroufly accompanied: but the mandate which the Guifes, iffued in the king's name, forbidding any other followers than their own houfehold; and the confidence which they repofed on their high rank, and relation to the royal blood, made them defpife and neglect thefe falutary precautions.—New informations and intimations the moſt alarming, met them on their way. They were affured, that Francis and his mother, intimidated by the impetuous counfels of the duke and cardinal, had been induced or compelled to adopt meafures the moſt fanguinary. The two princes, notwithſtanding, continued their journey. On their arrival, they entered the royal prefence, and faluted the king, who gave them a cold and un-

his inſtances to hers; and affured him of the good intentions of Francis. Thefe united efforts were at length fuccefsful. The princes reluctantly left Pau, and with a flender train proceeded towards Orleans.

gracious reception. The inftant of their departure, two captains of the guard took them into cuftody. Anthony was only carefully watched; but the prince of Condé was conducted to a houfe erected purpofely in a public fquare, and defended by fome pieces of cannon *.

The admiral was in Orleans at this time; but d'Andelot, more circumfpect,

* The marechal de Briffac firft propofed in council the prince's arreft. Francis figned the order, which was reluctantly counterfigned by the chancellor.
" I faw the two brothers, Anthony and Louis," fays Brantome, " when they arrived. The king
" entered the court of the palace on horfeback; the
" prince, on foot. Never did I fee a man exhibit
" a more bold and fearlefs mien than did the lat-
" ter; but on his return, when arrefted, he appeared
" covered with aftonifhment. Anthony, who had
" thought to difconcert and terrify his enemies by
" his menaces, and appearance at court, was not lefs
" confounded and amazed."

Davila very minutely defcribes their arrival at Orleans, the circumftances of the king's behaviour, and the queen-mother's pretended forrow on their arreft. He fays, both the princes were obliged to difmount without the gate.

and

and conscious of the danger, had retired into Bretagne.—The lady of Roye, mother to the princess of Condé, was arrested at her own chateau; and Grollot, bailiff of Orleans, was taken into custody.

Five judges, nominated to interrogate the prince, waited on him in prison for that purpose. In no degree dismayed by the violence exercised against him, he refused to plead before such a tribunal; and demanded a public trial by the whole parliament, peers, and king, as his dignity entitled him. This spirited and intrepid behaviour did not disconcert or delay his process. It was pursued uninterruptedly. He stood on the extreme verge of fate.—The Guises, already anticipating the sure destruction of this powerful rival, arrogant, and intoxicated with success, observed scarce any deference or decorum towards the queen-mother, whom they secretly suspected, and meant to divest of all influence or authority.—

Catherine faw the fatal error fhe had committed, in joining the princes of Lorrain, to her own injury, againſt, Anthony and Louis—but it was too late to retract. The evil was beyond a cure.—Grollot's condemnation and execution was univerfally regarded as preparatory to, and indicative of that of the prince :—when an unexpected and great event, big with the moſt important conſequences, ſnatched him from the imminent and impending deſtruction.

The king, to avoid the neceſſity of being preſent at the ſpectacle of Grollot's death, had gone out to the chace. On his return, he was attacked with a heavineſs in the head, which at the end of ſome days produced a ſuppurating abſceſs, with an impoſthume or fiſtula in his ear *. The ſymptoms did not at firſt appear

---

* Davila ſays, that " Francis, being under his
" barber's hands, was ſuddenly ſeized with an apo-
" plectic or fainting fit. His ſervants immediately
" laid him on the couch, without ſigns of life. He
" returned

appear alarming, or mortal; but the Guifes, apprehenfive of the event, and dreading left their prey fhould efcape, pufhed on the trial with unprecedented and indecent hafte. The cuftomary formalities, obferved in capital cafes, were omitted; and the prince finally condemned to lofe his head.

The chancellor, ever averfe to the violent meafures purfued, and feeing that Francis's malady grew more dangerous, artfully protracted his fignature to the arret for his execution. Of all the nobles and great perfonages with which the court was crowded—fo defpotic was the influence of the princes of Lorrain; fo abject the devotion paid them—that only the count de Sancerre had the courage to refufe to fign it, though three repeated orders of the king were brought him

---

" returned to his fenfes after fome time; but it was
" evident from the nature of the attack, and the
" effects it left on him, that he could not long
" furvive."

to that purpose. Whether Francis himself had fixed to it his sign manual or not, is a secret of state hidden, and never divulged.

Meanwhile the physicians, compelled by the nature of the symptoms they observed in the young king, declared him near his end. The Guises, conscious of the desperate and critical situation in which their conduct had involved them; and believing their own safety inseparably connected with a steady adherence to the principles which they had hitherto pursued, stood firm. Placing their reliance only in the prosecution of them, they endeavoured to induce Catherine to join them in arresting the king of Navarre *;

but

* Monsieur de Thou, that great historian, relates, that the duke of Guise had determined to put Anthony to death in Francis's presence, and had induced the deluded prince to consent to it. Though the king of Navarre received information of this infamous resolution, he had intrepidity enough to enter the apartment in which he was to be assassinated.—" If
" they

but she, too wise to be rendered subservient to their purposes—and freed from the tyranny they had exercised over her, by the prospect of Francis's death—refused to consent to, or permit his seizure. —She saw herself exactly in that situation to which she fondly aspired. The approaching minority left the regency open to her ambition. Both parties paid her the most assiduous court, as to the arbitress of their lives and fortunes. In the anticipation of her son's end, she took, with the most cool perspicuity and masterly address, the necessary precautions for securing to herself the first place in the government under Charles, immediate heir to the crown, and who

" they kill me," said he to Reinsy, one of his gentlemen, " carry my shirt, all bloody, to my wife and " son : they will read in my blood what they ought " to do to revenge it !"—Francis, shocked at the enormity of such a crime, did not dare to give the sign previously agreed on; and the duke of Guise, quitting the chamber, could not help exclaiming, " Le pauvre roi que nous avons !"

was only ten years and five months old. Anthony promifed in writing to cede to her the regency, which belonged to him of right, as firſt prince of the blood; and the Guifes fwore to ferve her in every manner, for and againſt whomever fhe commanded.

Amid thefe intrigues and cabals, Francis the fecond breathed his laſt, on the eighteenth day from his feizure, and aged only feventeen years ten months and a half. His reign was about a year and five months *.

We

* The critical nature of his death, fo opportune for the prefervation of the prince of Condé, fo fortunate to Catherine of Medecis, whom the Guifes had deprived of all influence, gave rife to reports of poifon. " Le Laboureur," and feveral other writers, have accufed Ambrofe Paré, the king's furgeon, and a Scotch valet de chambre, who was a Hugonot, with having poifoned his night-cap exactly at the place which anfwered to, and covered the fiftula in his ear: but De Thou, infinitely more worthy of credit, denies and difproves this affertion. He exprefly attributes his
death

We know not what qualities he poffeffed, or might have difcovered, had he attained to manhood. His capacity ap-

death to the weaknefs of his conftitution, and maladies
derived from his mother.

Davila feems to incline likewife to the belief, that
he died a natural death; yet he mentions the generally-
received opinion of his having been poifoned. " The
" young king," fays he, " had always been troubled
" with pains and defluxions in his head, from his in-
" fancy. An impofthume formed itfelf over his right
" ear; and that burfting, fo great a quantity of mat-
" ter fell into his throat, that it ftopped up the paf-
" fage, and prevented him either from fpeaking, or
" receiving any fort of nourifhment.—Moft peo-
" ple," continues Davila, " believed at the time, that
" his barber had conveyed poifon into his ear; and it
" was even reported, that the phyficians had difco-
" vered evident figns of it. The fuddennefs of
" Francis's feizure, and the extraordinary crifis in
" which he expired, would have given univerfal cre-
" dit to the accufation, if the diforder which termi-
" nated his life had not been known to have grown
" up with him from his cradle."

From the teftimonies of thefe two laft hiftorians,
we cannot hefitate to believe the king's death natural,
and almoft inevitable from his hereditary weaknefs and
complaints.

pears to have been very mean, and little superior to imbecillity, and his bodily infirmities added to thefe mental defects. Some French hiftorians have abfurdly given him the epithet of " The king " without vice." Voltaire has drawn his portrait more fpiritedly, and more juftly, in his Henriade.

" Foible enfant, qui de Guife adorait les ca-
" prices,
" Et dont on ignorait les vertus et les vices."

His chaftity has been made the fubject of encomium; but to the feeblenefs of his complexion, and early youth, this virtue may be chiefly attributed; befides that his attachment to his confort was extreme, and her beauty fuch as to challenge the warmeft homage of the heart.

Francis's funerals were indecently neglected. Ambition and intrigue occupied the whole court. Catherine, who had been oftentatioufly magnificent in the obfequies of her hufband, was equally remifs in thofe of her fon. The Guifes, on whom he had heaped so many favours, to whom he had confided such unlimited power, by a conduct which marked them with the basest ingratitude, did not shew him this last and poor token of respect. They excused themselves under the frivolous pretext of remaining to console the young queen, their niece.

Among so many lords and bishops as were at Orleans, only Sansac and La Brosse, who had been his governors, and Guillard bishop of Senlis, who was blind, followed his corpse to St. Denis.—Upon the cloth which covered his coffin, a billet was found, containing this severe and pointed sarcasm. " Tanneguy du Chatel, " où es tu ?"—It alluded to the funeral rites of Charles the seventh.—Du Chatel had been that monarch's favourite, but was banished from court. At his death, he generously returned, and, as a mark of his gratitude and affection to a master.he had loved, performed his funerals at his private expence, with a royal pomp.

Francis

Francis the second left no iſſue, legitimate or illegitimate, and the crown deſcended to Charles his brother.——Mary, queen of France and Scotland, makes no figure in her huſband's reign. Subſervient to, and awed by the daring genius of her uncles, ſhe performed only an inferior part. They made uſe of her charms and influence over the young king, to bend him to their wiſhes and meaſures. In a court of ſuch gallantry, where her beauty was adored, ſhe could not eſcape ſome malignant and falſe reflections on her conduct; but they do not deſerve to be mentioned, much leſs to be refuted.

The conſtable, who had been repeatedly ordered to Orleans, but whoſe diſtruſt and caution rendered him ſlow, accelerated his march on the news of the king's death *. He arrived on the third day after

* Davila, uſually ſo exact, and on whoſe authority we may rely with an almoſt implicit faith, expreſly aſſerts, " That the prince of Condé was con-
" demned to be beheaded before the royal palace,
" previous

after that event, accompanied by fix hundred horfe; and, making ufe of the authority which his charge gave him, drove the guards from the gates of the city; threatening to hang them up, if they kept the king invefted, in full peace, and in the centre of his kingdom.

Meanwhile the prince of Condé efcaped, amid thefe unexpected changes. Francis's death unloofed his fetters. With a magnanimity and courage becoming himfelf, he notwithftanding refufed to quit his prifon, till he knew who had been his profecutors and accufers. No

" previous to Francis the fecond's feizure; and that
" the execution of the fentence was only delayed, in
" hopes to draw Montmorenci and his fons into the
" net, and to involve the king of Navarre in the fame
" common deftruction." So that the conftable's delays were chiefly inftrumental to Condé's prefervation. It is impoffible not to be amazed at the bold and nearly fuccefsful plan of the duke and cardinal, thus at one blow to cut off, by a folemn and public trial, two princes of the blood, and the firft officer of the crown.

person dared avow himself as such. The Guises declared that every step had been taken by the late king's express and particular command; but they did not produce the royal order, in consequence of which measures so violent had been pursued. Thirteen days afterwards the prince quitted Orleans, accompanied, as a mark of honour, by those very soldiers who had served as his guard, and retired to Ham in Picardy.

END OF THE FIRST VOLUME.

www.ingramcontent.com/pod-product-compliance
Lightning Source LLC
Chambersburg PA
CBHW022118290426
44112CB00008B/723